WRITING YOURSELF AWAKE

MEDITATION & CREATIVITY

Kimberley Snow

Many thanks to those who helped to make this book a reality: Dan Gerber, Chryss Yost, David Starkey, Rachel Altman, Molly Green, and the late Barry Spacks.

BLUESTONE BOOKS
SANTA BARBARA, CA

DEDICATION

To those who aspire to wake up and to those,
past and present, who have helped us to do so.

CONTENTS

MEDITATION, MINDFULNESS & CONTEMPLATION.

BECOMING MORE EMOTIONALLY AWARE 51

INTRODUCTION

This volume offers a natural follow up to my book *Writing Yourself Home* which grew out of my involvement with Women's Studies and focused on actualizing the self. *Writing Yourself Awake,* written after a decade of being deeply immersed in Buddhism, combines meditation with writing, exploring deeper levels of the self and connecting the personal to the world beyond. Its techniques are based on a wide range of methods, tested and expanded through a series of dharma workshops and study groups. These classes included both meanings of the term dharma—the teachings of the Buddha and the way things are.

"Don't write. No notes. Just listen," a Tibetan teacher once told our group during a retreat. Heads bent over our notebooks, we wrote down, "Don't write. No notes. Just listen."

If we'd been educated in the oral tradition of Tibet, we'd have been able to hear the teachings and remember them, but we'd all been raised in a culture largely geared toward the written word. We'd grown up taking notes, making lists, even writing in the margins of books. A large part of our learning came through the act of writing itself, as if the moving hand were an extension of the brain. We seem to be hard-wired to remember things written down and/or seen on a page more easily than something simply heard.

Although not part of the traditional Buddhist path, personal writing provides a natural way for Westerners to explore and integrate deep teachings. Writing can become a form of meditation itself, a support for mindfulness, and an effective method for unraveling and recording insights.

My approach is to provide more suggestions, writing prompts, and queries than any one person could need. Surely a few of these will relate to you and be helpful to your particular situation. Use these provocations for yourself or as the basis of a meditation-writing group. Think of them as a sort of cookbook -- dip in here and there until you find an appropriate choice.

In the following pages, the focus is not on crafting or editing writing, but on the process of writing itself and how it can be integrated with meditation, mindfulness and contemplation to bring about small and large shifts in consciousness. The writing itself benefits, of course, for creativity is enhanced and imagination is unleashed as the fixations that limit us begin to dissolve. The focus here is on how to use writing to deepen awareness, and be more in touch with ourselves and others in a more authentic way, one aligned with remaining awake and aware by coming to see things just as they are.

WRITING AND MEDITATION

We have to be careful not to think that meditation is about getting rid of thoughts. On the contrary, I would say that meditation helps us to creatively engage with our thoughts and not fixate on them.

~Martine Batchelor

Rather than seeing mindfulness and Buddhism as shaping my efforts on the page, what I've come to understand is that my lifelong pursuit of writing and creativity has helped to open me to the path of Buddhism.

~ Dinty W. Moore

Kimberley Snow

WRITING

> In order to write we must have an awareness of who we are—and who we aren't. If you don't know either, writing can help teach it.
>
> ~Natalie Goldberg

Writing releases us into a timeless world where all things are possible. Through the play of our imagination, we gain the power to expand our limits, to integrate change and to guide our personal growth. In this magical realm, we can reclaim past events, retrieve former selves, live out what almost was, what could have been. Through writing and visualization we are able to develop a personal language that fills out the hollows and blank spaces in our lives, to make sense of and give reality to our experience. In this private arena where conscious and unconscious meet and interact, we are granted a unique opportunity to negotiate peace settlements between inner and outer, between self and other. In short, to create and maintain core happiness through a time-honored method that is not only free but non-caloric as well.

MEDITATION

Meditation is one of those words like cooking that covers many different activities from baking to braising to frying to boiling. There are meditations to produce relaxation, to focus attention, to develop compassion, or to enhance clarity and awareness, to mention just a few. As in cooking, meditation is designed to create some sort of change through its processes.

In the most basic meditations, we simply learn to turn the mind that usually goes outward to look inward instead. We are able to get under the hood of our own minds, so to speak, to glimpse inner workings. By taking up meditation, we don't lose the ability to navigate and understand the outside world. Far from it, as we withdraw our projections from the outer sphere, it comes into clearer focus, revealing what is actually there.

WHY COMBINE WRITING & MEDITATION?

As both a writer and meditator, over the years I have found that the more I meditate, the more insight I bring to my writing and the deeper I can go into the process. Paradoxically, I found that meditation allowed me to be more creative and spontaneous when writing and to enjoy the process of playing with words. Through leading workshops, I discovered that this holds true for others as well.

My poet husband often used to say that his poetry turned out to be smarter than he was, and that his poems frequently became his dharma guides. I've found that as my fictional characters find ways to loosen the grip of self-involvement and align themselves toward others, so do I.

As meditators we both found that writing itself is enormously helpful in integrating the insights from sitting practice and incorporating them into our daily lives. Writing is especially useful in sorting out the messy stuff that comes up during practice.

To progress on a path, it's often a question of getting out of our own way in order to function with compassionate awareness, and to release ourselves from the grip of destructive emotions, especially fear. Sometimes if we come at feelings and events sideways through poetry or fiction rather than head-on, we are able to bring more gentleness and self awareness into the process. By telling all the truth but telling it slant as Emily Dickinson suggests, we can often come to understand an old situation with startling clarity.

It's natural that both writing and meditating work so well in tandem with each other. Both are seeking what's real, what's authentic. Through meditation we come to see reality as it is; through writing we learn to find ways to live comfortably with things as they are.

AWAKENING

It is through conscious individual existence that the developing consciousness becomes organized and capable to awaken into its own reality.
~Sri Aurobindo

What are we waking up from? Let's call it the daze of the isolated, reactive, limited self. What are we waking into? A larger, more easeful world, where things are not fixed, but flow.

In the human default mode, before self-awareness kicks in, we are constantly talking to ourselves in an almost compulsive fashion. This happens without us being able to stop it, nor can we turn it off. It's like watching TV when someone else has the remote. Not only that, but we get caught up in our thoughts and assessments, we become fused with them as though they represent the true nature of reality. The thinking process of an untrained mind tends to be obsessive, compulsive, and generally inaccurate for it assumes that every thought is true just because we think it. Emotionally, we go through our days reacting to others and situations automatically, without much self knowledge about why we are responding in the ways we do. Furthermore, we feel that we need to protect and defend our sense of self, gradually building up a wall around ourselves. This isn't a moral failing on our part, it is nobody's fault. It's just the way our minds work until they are directed to do otherwise.

There are a wide variety of methods for training the mind. Many of the techniques in this book grow out of secular Buddhist psychology or nature of mind teachings. You don't have to become a Buddhist (or anything else) to get the most out of them. Nor do you have to be an aspiring writer to take advantage of the parts of the book that have to do with writing. If you don't like to write, simply contemplate instead. These methods are available to anyone inspired to change in a positive direction.

One of the results of being more conscious is to see things just as they are—not nearly as grim as it sounds. In fact, it is a very good thing since in reality we're far more than we now imagine. We are capable of developing core happiness, able to connect authentically with others in a kind and compassionate way, and to live richly with an opened heart. Being awake means being free of bewilderment and a nagging sense of unease that comes from constantly defending a limited sense of self that keeps us isolated. The payoffs of aligning ourselves with the dharma are enormous, almost unimaginable when we first begin. But slowly, slowly we begin to change in fundamental ways, not unlike an ice cube in warm water.

SIMILARITIES OF WRITING & MEDITATION

Both writing and meditation are ways to expand and enrich time. In meditation, we learn to examine our thoughts and feelings from a new perspective, to watch the river of our consciousness flow by, observing it but not attaching ourselves to it. We train ourselves to have a meta-consciousness that observes ourselves observing, and that enlarges moments into infinity. In writing, we also develop that meta-consciousness. We experience our lives as lived events, but also as material to be carefully examined later for richness and meaning. Just as meditation makes life more aware and joyous, so writing allows us to live more deeply and fully. Both involved the sanctification of time.

~Mary Pipher

Many have found that people in therapy get well quicker if they also do mindfulness meditation. Writing also improves with meditation, no matter if you are journaling, writing poetry or prose. The similarities are stronger during the writing process than the editing and publishing phase. Initially, however, we find many similarities.

- Both provide ways of making friends with yourself – of connecting with yourself emotionally in a positive way.

- Both provide ways of understanding and transforming the self through insight.

- Both strive to make the unconscious conscious by requiring that you develop introspection on a deep level.

- Both evoke an inner dialogue that you know to be authentic.

- Both allow you to become a witness to your life – past and present – not just to react to it.

- Both can lead toward a new level of personal integration.

- Both involve being embodied – the physical, mental and emotional are all involved.

- Both are committed to finding out what is true.

- Both are full of surprises and revelations.

- Both may include flat, dull phases where nothing seems to be happening.

- Both tap into a deeper source of intelligence or intuition if you don't give up.

- Both can generate insight into the way the mind works, the nature of the self, the truth of your relationships with others and your place in the world.

- Both involve going into a unique mind-space.

- Both require courage. To seek what lies beneath is not for sissies.

- Both include a learning curve.

- Both progress through a variety of phases. Each phase has different challenges and rewards.

- Both include possible wrong directions, false starts, and blind alleys.

- Both improve if you do them long enough.

- Both can induce performance anxiety and/or guilt and feelings of inadequacy.

- Both can often cause resistance to scheduling. If you think you are supposed to meditate for 24 minutes every day or write for 15 minutes, you often might have trouble getting started. Once you begin, you're often glad that you did, but at times the resistance can be very strong. 15 mmm

- Both are ways to ultimately connect with the world although we usually meditate and write alone.

- Both allow us to witness our life, not just react to it.

- Both have had many books written about them with lots of advice on how to proceed, but in the end you have to learn how to do them yourself, have to rely on your own inner wisdom and intuition.

- Both can bring genuine happiness.

- For both you have to pay attention, show up, be present, embodied.

WRITING FROM DEEP MIND

Traditionally Westerners have sought happiness and solutions to problems outside the self, focusing on the material and physical universe. The mind goes out to make sense of the world and has gotten extremely good at it. In the East, there is more of a tendency to look inward to see how the mind works, to investigate the deeper levels of consciousness to uncover what we can do or stop doing that will allow us to live a happier and more productive life.

Buddhist psychology describes *sem* or ordinary mind as being like the choppy waves on the surface of the ocean. Our minds are constantly busy with thoughts incessantly tumbling over thoughts, always coming and going, always changing. Below sem is a different type of awareness and intelligence although it is all part of the same ocean. This deep mind is called by many names such as pristine awareness and natural mind, and is seen as the source of creativity, insight and wisdom. These deeper levels are traditionally accessed through meditation.

In calm abiding meditation (Shamatha) one follows the breath, in and out, in and out. Since you can't breathe in the past or the future, this teaches you to keep returning to the present moment. In turn, one develops relaxation, stability and clarity. Once these qualities have been established through sustained calm abiding meditation, small gaps begin to appear in the layer of obsessive thoughts, fearfulness, and compulsive ideation that we take as normal reality. As we learn to rest in these gaps for longer periods of time, our fears, grasping, and aversions begin to become more and more transparent and relax their grip on us. In time, our mind learns to relax into what is often called its natural state, which is open, luminous, and spontaneously present. In the resultant open space, positive emotions such as loving kindness and compassion arise spontaneously, and begin gradually to crowd out negative or counterproductive ones. The luminous aspect of the natural state brings cognitive insight "like a flash of lightning on a dark night." Once the jabbering brain with its constant planning and worrying is silenced, true wisdom can begin to emerge.

Engaging the Imagination

> From the point of view of the rationally organized world, imagination is dangerous, for it holds that world in supreme irony, as a mere backdrop for its colorful activity. No wonder Plato wanted to exclude the poets from his Republic. And no wonder religion almost always mistrusts and fears the imagination, which is forever evoking energies—sexual and creative energies—religion would just as soon forget: they are just so messy and hard to control, and they are not usually polite.
>
> ~Norman Fischer

Art, Norman Fischer reminds us, can save us from freezing. It warms and melts us, creates flow. We freeze our sense of self and the world in order to control it or at least make it feel less chaotic. Unfortunately we often use spiritual practice to aid and abet this freezing process even though it is designed to do just the opposite.

Imagination reveals things that are often hidden by analytical thinking, it surprises us with insights and new ways of awareness. It is our friend in a way that our conceptual mind isn't. The conceptual mind works for the ego, strives to keep things in order, fixed, in safe boxes. The imagination operates free lance. Wild and irreverent, it's more fun, more spontaneous, full of surprises. It can turn around and bite you as well, just as you feel you have everything under control. Especially when you are congratulating yourself on having it all together. As it does in dreams, sometimes in meditation and often in the writing process, the imagination finds a side door, an open window, a pin hole, to slip through and mix things up, break up the ice, let things flow.

WRITING TO PROMPTS

Writing to prompts engages the imagination in ways that are mysterious but often effective. Adrenalin pumps, the imagination perks up, the battened down hatches creak open. The logical, analytical mind is momentarily shoved aside, and you're off, released.

Prompts and suggestions abound in this book. No one could possibly be expected to respond to all or even a fraction of those provided, but just reading a prompt or a question might plant a seed or set off a spark in your own mind. Some people may prefer contemplation to actual writing. Use the prompts to keep the door to the imagination ajar in whatever way you wish. Let them inspire you to write something else or to ask a different question. Argue with them, poke around to see what lies underneath, be curious about their effect. Whatever works.

ENHANCING CREATIVITY

You get your intuition back when you make space for it, when you stop the chattering of the rational mind. The rational mind doesn't nourish you. You assume that it gives you the truth, because the rational mind is the golden calf that this culture worships, but this is not true. Rationality squeezes out much that is rich and juicy and fascinating.

~Anne Lamott

SEE THINGS JUST AS THEY ARE

Go outside. Walk around and look at things in themselves. Don't let your mind wander. If you see a rose, for instance, don't trip out on the roses you received, the roses you sent. Just see the rose. Don't think about which vase it will look best in. Don't think about aphids. Just see.

CALM DOWN AND RELAX THE MIND

Creativity needs space.

Creativity springs spontaneously from deep mind. It's there, to be released when the shut door swings open.

Sometimes you have to stop doing something (fixating for instance) to let creativity through. It's a gradual process.

Calm Abiding meditation that focuses on relaxation, stability and clarity is a good way to start. First relax: scan the body for tension, paying attention to physical sensations. Begin to follow the breath, in and out, in and out. Count if it helps. Inhale, count one, exhale; inhale, count two, exhale. Go to five. The point isn't to count but to stabilize the mind. Drop the counting when you don't need it anymore. You also need to stabilize the body as well as the mind: don't fidget or wiggle—stay still as a mountain. Clarity comes when you keep remembering to follow the breath, when you remain aware of what you are doing.

LEARN TO DEAL WITH FEAR

> Fear is created not by the world around us, but in the mind, by what we think is going to happen.

~Elisabeth Gawain

Much of releasing creativity has to do with getting rid of fear. Fear squeezes us shut, cuts us off from deep mind, freezes our spontaneous selves.

Fear of writing exists on many different levels. As in public speaking, there is the fear of being judged, being exposed, being out there. There is the fear of failure, fear of success (so they say).

Memorize this and recite it when needed:

Bene Gesserit Litany Against Fear

> I must not fear. Fear is the mind-killer.
> Fear is the little-death that brings total obliteration.
> I will face my fear.
> I will permit it to pass over me and through me.
> And when it has gone past
> I will turn the inner eye to see its path.
> Where the fear has gone there will be nothing.
> Only I will remain.

Frank Herbert, *Dune*

Also see the section on fear in the Emotional Awareness section of this book.

OPEN THE HEART

> The wisdom of the heart can be found in any circumstance, on any planet, round or square. It arises not through knowledge or images of perfection or by comparison and judgment, but by seeing with the eyes of wisdom and the heart of loving attention, by touching with compassion all that exists in our world.
>
> ~Jack Kornfield

When writing about others, don't just stick with your own thoughts about them, try to see others from inside their minds, walk in their shoes. Make them a subject rather than an object, develop empathy by telling their story.

Imagine yourself in different difficult situations. Start with old age, sickness and death.

Loving kindness meditation: connect with that part of yourself where everything feels okay. A little spark of all-rightness. Feel it in the heart area. Just connect with it gently, don't pounce on it. In a traditional loving kindness meditation, you send this feeling throughout your own body, soak in it, then send it out to others.

PROMPT: Write about someone in a nursing home. Someone who is alone, afraid. Swallowing her pride, she calls her daughter in another city. What happens then?

Pick a story from the news of someone in a difficult situation. Contemplate the immediate and long-term implications of what it might mean to be in that situation.

READ MORE POETRY

> ... You can say anything you want, yessir, but it's the words that sing, they soar and descend ... I bow to them ... I love them, I cling to them, I run them down, I bite into them, I melt them down ... I love words so much ... The unexpected ones ... The ones I wait for greedily or stalk until, suddenly, they drop ... Vowels I love ... They glitter like colored stones, they leap like silver fish, they are foam, thread, metal, dew ... I run after certain words ... They are so beautiful that I want to fit them all into my poem .. I catch them in mid-flight, as they buzz past, I trap them, clean them, peel them, I set myself in front of the dish, they have a crystalline texture to me, vibrant, ivory, vegetable, oily, like fruit, like algae, like agates, like olives ... And then I stir them, I shake them, I drink them, I gulp them down, I mash them, I garnish them, I let them go...

~Pablo Neruda

Prose goes in a straight line. Takes you from point A to Point B, then on to C. No such luck with poetry. It's non-convergent, liable to take you places you never considered going. It doesn't care.

Poetry often says things that you can't comprehend. You have to go a little sideways to understand. Even then it makes sense in another dimension somehow, not this one.

Writing a poem is a highly creative endeavor, but so is reading one. Poetry exists at the edge of the campfire circle, there where the light meets the dark, where the known gives way to the unknown. Jump into a poet's mind and let it take you away, lead you astray.

USE YOUR SENSES

> Part of the work of finding your own deep writing comes from awareness of the body. It's easy for us to forget the importance of the body in the writing process. . . . Our cells have memories. Our bodies have stored all of our experiences—those expressed and unexpressed, even those forgotten. They are there, waiting for us.
>
> ~Laraine Herring

Some writing seems to take place in an unfurnished, unventilated room, located somewhere in midair. There's no juice to the writing. Only ideas.

The senses don't have to be described in the writing (no "the lushness of the cream on the tongue" sort of thing) so much as to be part of the overall open awareness of the writer.

Do this:

Smell a rose.

Stroke a piece of velvet, a suede coat, a cat.

Eat a piece of crystallized ginger (or ginger snap) tiny bit by tiny bit. Or a raisin if you don't like ginger. Taste it thoroughly, completely. Note your reactions to food in your mouth. Is it to hurry to swallow it so you can eat more? What happens when you slow down and truly experience each morsel?

Sing your next thought.

Meditation with an object: place your attention on an external object. It can be anything, from a computer mouse to a holy relic. Rather than bringing your attention back to your breath as you normally would, let it return gently to rest on the object with bare attention.

The next time you meditate, pay attention to sounds. Focus on each sound as it arises, abides, disappears. Note your reaction to the sounds, the way in which the mind is taken away by thoughts, memory, and reactions. When the sound of a siren comes into the meditation, do you react with aversion? Can you just hear it as sound waves hitting your ear drum without wanting to push it away?

As a writer, visualize your characters in detail, color of hair, eyes, the way they move, what they are wearing. What do they themselves smell as they interact with the world? How open are their senses?

Eavesdrop on random conversations and listen to speech rhythms, tone. Create a distinctive voice for each of your characters, speak it out.

Describe a vivid landscape through use of specific details, use photographs as well as your own memory for inspiration.

LIGHTEN UP

For a quick intervention: Stop. Relax the muscles of the face, they can hold a lot of tension. Even quicker: smile, laugh, chortle. This relaxes the muscles in your face very rapidly and keeps you from feeling so grim about things.

TRUST YOUR INTUITION

> The moment you find a technique, you become attached to it and there is no longer any open listening. The mind clings to methods because it finds safety in them. Real questioning has no methods, no knowing—just wondering freely, vulnerably, what it is that is actually happening inside and out. Not the word, not the idea of it, not the reaction to it, but the simple fact.

~Toni Packer

Writing often begins as a one-way street and gradually develops into a two way street. (From '*I* want to write' to 'writing'). To start getting energy from the writing, let your words trickle down into an area of unknowing. This part of the mind is often more imaginative than you are. Sink into it through dreams, through meditation, through letting go.

Make "Let it be" a constant part of the process.

WRITE A POEM

Don't think of yourself as a poet? Feel that poetry is beyond you? Afraid that you don't understand it at all? All the more reason to write a poem.

The following advice on how to begin is from poet Barry Spacks:

Start by reading poetry—aloud, if possible—by contemporaries, those who can fill your consciousness with the sounds and subjects, the diction, thought, rhythms and reference, of our own wacky times.

Next, take a vow not to rhyme. Just at the beginning. Why? Because playing with rhyme when you're starting out may keep you busy skimming the surface instead of plunging to some personal depth. There will be plenty of time later to toss off a cute limerick or sweat over a sonnet or sestina.

Here's an exercise that many have found helpful. It works against blockage by asking you to start and end with arbitrary lines. The crucial tool is not a rhyming dictionary nor a metronome nor rules of any kind. Just the opposite. What's needed is relaxation and a willingness to leap off cliffs, verbally speaking.

EXERCISE:

Step one: pick one of the following as your first line and start writing:

> (1) When I am calm
>
> (2) I love you madly, sure, and yet
>
> (3) Judgments tap-dancing my buzzy brain
>
> (4) Dear Buddha, am I becoming worthy
>
> (5) Once past hope and fear

(6) A little child shall lead the way

(7) Inspired by how the Buddha sits

(8) An eagle poised upon a cliff

(9) What prevents? a frozen root?

(10) Polishing the silence

Please don't worry about the quality of insight, the lilt, the turn of phrase. Later you can brood over word-choice, rhythm, symbol, cutting away the dead parts, making changes, rearranging, developing ideas. Now you simply want to keep going. Continuing will lead you somewhere, maybe to tears, to surprise if you're lucky. But those new to this "rolling on" will usually go dry, often rather soon. You'll find you're slowing down, through a disinclination or inability to go any further. Aha, now comes tricky step two of the exercise.

Step two: take one of the first lines you didn't choose -- or any line at all! -- and jot it at the bottom of the page. Continue developing what you've written so far with the intent to finish on the newly chosen last line while making some kind of sense.

See what you're doing here in step two? You're combining the arbitrary—even the zany—with a degree of meaningfulness. Step two of the exercise wants to lead you to the exploratory work of "thinking like a poet" by forging connecting links to bring this little ticking machine of a poem to a halt with a sense of closure on just the arbitrary last line you've chosen.

Obviously, once you're finished with your draft you're free to change these words, maybe remove them altogether like the scaffolding of a finished building. You're the boss of your poem.

Now it's time to look the page over and throw away everything not to your liking. You may be left with only a line, a phrase, that sings, that you find truly interesting, or you may have tricked yourself into a whole sequence displaying that quality of especially fresh and moving language we call poetry. (Once, doing this exercise, I crossed out all but two words before I started again.)

You may want to begin a second draft attempting to weave together the lines you like from draft number one with subject matter the exercise may have helped you find. Writing a poem is a voyage of discovery. In fact, supplying your own first and last lines in future will provide a method of composition that could keep you writing poems for a lifetime.

DON'T RESIST WHATEVER COMES UP

We shield our heart with an armor woven out of very old habits of pushing away pain and grasping at pleasure. We push away what's unwanted and grasp what's wanted. When you begin to breathe in the pain instead of pushing it away, you begin to open your heart to what's unwanted. When we relate directly in this way to the unwanted areas of our lives, the small, dark room of ego begins to be ventilated.

~Pema Chodron

Don't resist ideas or emotions as they arise. Write them out, edit later. Just be curious about them, investigate them. Watch them. Name them, turn them into characters. Try to understand what they need, what they want.

EXERCISE: Breathe mindfully for a few minutes. Set your intention to not stop whatever comes up in your meditation. Make the thoughts that arise the focus of your mediation rather than following the breath. Just watch them as they arise in the space of the mind. Don't try to manipulate them in any way, just give them bare attention. Let them arise, abide, and dissolve.

WRITING: Imagine a bus coming toward you. The bus stops and different people begin to get off. These are personifications of elements from your recent meditation. Each of them wears a distinctive hat. Describe their hats. Give them names and physical descriptions. Pay special attention to their eyes.

WRITE ANOTHER POEM

Maybe a short one. Start with one if these words:

Remember

Imagine

Don't

Let's

Please

Someday

Forget

ONE WORD CONTEMPLATION

This is adapted from a Zen technique and is most effective if you use a calligraphy pen, stylus and India ink, or brush and paint. Even a gel pen will work.

Find a quiet spot. Sit quietly for a few minutes. Take several deep breaths.

Pick a single word that embodies a subject you wish to contemplate such as impermanence, interdependence, love, relationship, etc.

Keeping your attention on both your breath and on the stroke, begin to write the word, forming each letter as if it were calligraphy. Move very deliberately, keeping your mind on the task at hand. Follow the pen as you would follow the breath, without distraction, remaining present, concentrating on the task at hand.

When finished, contemplate the word by sinking into a reverie about its implications, deeper meaning.

Simply look at the word and allow associations to arise spontaneously, then gently return your attention to the word itself.

WRITE A PLAY

Plays—even if only a few pages long—can be a great deal of fun to write. They are like extended poems in that they rely on voice and timing. Writing a one-act play with a single setting is the quickest, easiest way to learn the craft. It's simple, really. Fun. Except for a description of the set, list of characters, and a few stage directions, the whole thing consists of dialogue.

Rather than the novelist dialogue of:

"I don't know," Bibi sighed, putting down the legal papers he had just handed her on the ivory inlaid table beside her. She looked wistfully out the window where the winter-bare trees appeared slightly yellow in the fading light.

"I do," her husband John replied, looking at her coldly, realizing again how much she was starting to remind him of his mother. "Know."

It becomes:

Bibi: I don't know. (PUTS DOWN PAPERS HE HAS HANDED HER)

John: I do. Know.

It's the job of the actors and the director to carry the meaning of this scene in a play, rather than the narrative supplied by the writer. It's a fascinating form. A play can be only a few pages long but needs to show conflict and resolution through dialogue.

GOOD ADVICE: If you want to learn to write dialogue, write a one-act play or turn something that you've been working on into a play. If writing from a novel or story, you can always go back and insert the he-saids and she-replieds, but there is something about externalizing a story into play form that clarifies it, and adds zing. Works like magic.

WRITING: *Set a scene in a small zendo or meditation center. The roshi or teacher comes into the room where five students are sitting. He says he has an announcement to make. What is it? Who are the others? How do the others react? What tensions develop between the teacher and the students, among the students?*

Write a two person play featuring you and the Buddha. It begins with you asking the Buddha a question. Or vice-versa. What is the question? The answer?

Write a short one-person play with your mother as the main character—in which she is talking mainly about you.

RELAX THE MIND

Alternate writing with relaxing the mind.

Write until you start to give out, then meditate for about ten minutes Simply sit. Breathe.

If you are feeling speedy, breathe through the belly, expanding the abdomen, and holding each breath for a short time, then a long release.

If your mind is feeling cramped, go outside and take 21 deep breaths. Look at the sky. Breathe out your mind and keep it there.

After the breathing, simply relax the mind, rest in a state of awareness without center, without circumference.

Stretch.

Go back to writing.

Repeat as needed.

WRITE BADLY

Being interfered with by your inner critic? Try this:

Write as badly as you can. Use every awkward construction, vague reference, or unclear concept you wish. Pile it on. Go on to double negatives, dangling modifiers, split infinitives. Lay into verbs that don't agree, references that don't connect, and the passive voice without end. Write across the margins and upside down on the page. Write until you like the feel of the pen in your hand, until you are having fun. Repeat this exercise every time you sense you are not in control of your writing.

EXPLORE FLASH FICTION

Flash fiction is close to poetry in that it is about using words economically. Flash fiction pieces run from 100 to 1000 words and stress minimalism or bare-bones writing. Unlike poetry, metaphors or similes find less of a home here. Flash fiction is something like a short story or novel for today's readers with short little attention spans. It has a beginning, middle and end. It tells a story and includes characters, but there is a grey-area overlap between prose poems and flash fiction.

Flash fiction can be especially useful to the dharma student in that a "sudden glimpse" of insight can be expressed quickly.

Example:

The Man in the Buddha Tee Shirt

He's a big good-looking fellow, the Man in the Buddha tee shirt.

No day will go past when he'd consider failing us, Buddha-wise.

Each midnight he washes the tee shirt in question in sink suds, then wrings it out, supplies a garment-snap producing water-mist—satisfying moment—the tee then stretched out flat on a thick towel to dry, at morning a little touch-up by iron, that's it.

The tee shirt wearer also favors khaki pants and is partial to sockless running shoes. Apparently he has no need for a regular job. No, instead he plays the beggar on State Street at Anapamu, so I've been told.

He sports no sign—DOUGH FOR BREAD, that sort of thing—and he sets out no cup for coin. He doesn't solicit or entertain, he's a shirt-and-smile man and that's it.

Rarely folks come up close to offer succor, taking him for a needy homeless (we know he's not homeless from the way he washes the tee shirt). Such charity-oriented folks may press a dollar bill into his hand, where else would they put it?

He'll tilt his head then wisely and tuck the charity dollar bill into his left pants pocket, then dip from his right a money-stash the shape of a rolled-up pair of socks, a big roll of fives. He'll slip off a fiver and hold that out to the charity One-Buck Chuck. Now what? Catch Chuck's confusion on You-Tube. For Chuck has come unstuck, bedazzled, strange, wuz up? A frozen instant. He offered a One and in return comes a Five. Several such exchanges transpire daily, kensho's, mini-Satori's, for a certain sort of teaching is going on. The Buddha-shirt-man speaks not a word. His benefactors go: "huh? wha'? I thought... whoa!...you sure? Weird."

Giving is good. Pass it on.

Barry Spacks, Online Journal: *Cease, Cows*

Experiment with the form. Start with an interesting idea or insight character. Think in terms of conflict, dialogue, action and resolution.

FREE THE BODY

Don't forget that you have a body. Try to stay in it or at least visit it from time to time. Exercise at your desk, stretch. Work the hands: extend the fingers, clench them into fists, then relax the whole hand.

Scan the body for tension, note physical sensations. Breathe into the tight spots.

Get up and walk around. Do yoga stretches.

Tai Chi Hand Exercise:

While standing, visualize a largish wheel in front of you, with the rim facing you. With your hands on either side of the wheel, several inches apart, begin to circle the rim. Keeping the hands in tandem, continue to circle until you can feel the energy begin to build up between your palms. Go faster. When your palms tingle with energy, pick up a pen and start to write.

Dance.

Hop backwards.

Try to kiss your elbow.

Try to put your foot in your mouth.

Sit back down and write.

BREATHE IN THE WORLD

> Breath is the bridge which connects life to consciousness,
> which unites your body to your thoughts. Whenever your
> mind becomes scattered, use your breath as the means to
> take hold of your mind again.
>
> ~Thich Nhat Hanh

Go out into nature and breathe in the elements. Feel them enter your body, displacing fixation and neurosis.

Stand in the sun and breathe in the warmth of the fire element.

Sit on the ground and feel the solid energy of the earth element as you breathe it in.

Stand in the ocean, a river, pond or puddle. Experience the sense of flow in the water.

Watch the wind blow through trees or as it ripples the surface of water. Let the movement of air fill your body.

Find an unobstructed spot and look at the space of the sky. Breathe it in, letting it expand the mind into sky.

BE PRESENT

Align with the present moment. You can't breathe in the past or the future, so stop and just breathe for a few minutes. In and out. In and out. Don't call it meditation. Just sit and breathe. Keep coming back to the present. Be here. Now.

MEDITATION: Sit and breathe for a few minutes. Ask yourself: "I wonder what my next thought will be?"

The question generally creates a tiny awakening, a little gap between thoughts, a minute glimpse into the present moment.

MEDITATION

MINDFULNESS

&

CONTEMPLATION

Meditating means bringing the mind back to something again and again. Thus, we all meditate, but unless we direct it in some way, we meditate on ourselves and on our own problems, reinforcing our self-clinging.

~Lama Yeshe Dorje

Meditation allows us to directly participate in our lives instead of living life as an afterthought.

~Stephen Levine

TYPES OF MEDITATION PRACTICE

Meditation is not a means to an end. It is both the means and the end."

~J. Krishnamurti

Meditation means "to become familiar with," so we are always meditating on something. Breakfast. Our clothes. This guy we just met. That girl. Often we're fixating on the negative: What someone did wrong at work. How our mother/daughter/father/son/wife/husband fails to understand us, does not support our needs, is generally lacking. These can often be lengthy meditations indeed. So the question is whether our meditation is doing anything for us or just working to deepen unfortunate patterns. By taking up traditional meditation, we develop an intention of where our attention is being placed and an awareness of our motivation for doing so. In this way, we align ourselves with positive change.

Basic calm abiding meditation conditions the mind to pay attention, to become conscious of bodily sensations such as breathing, and to be comfortable staying in the present. It slows us down and opens a space for mindfulness.

Another practice in traditional meditation, variously called introspection or contemplation or insight, begins to shed light into how the human mind works. It can be quite profound and life changing and lead to a paradigm shift in ways that following the breath cannot. If you only follow the breath, it is like pausing a tape, but when you get up from the cushion, you're right back at the same point before you paused. Nothing has really changed in terms of changing negative patterns although your stress may be reduced.

Wisdom teachings and contemplation need to be added to relaxation meditation for deep changes to take place. But first, one needs to learn to stabilize the attention which is the cornerstone of all other mindfulness practices.

How to Meditate

> Although meditation is actually very simple, it is easy to get confused by the many different descriptions of meditative practices. Forget them all and just sit quietly.
>
> ~Tarthang Tulku

Calm abiding meditation focuses on following the breath, in and out, in and out, in a natural rhythm. This meditation trains us to keep coming back to the present moment. It also fosters relaxation, stability, and clarity.

In any meditation, it helps to sit up straight so that the air flows freely through body. First just sit. Don't try to do anything. Just sit. Next comes relaxation: become aware of the muscle groups in the face, the forehead, around the eyes, the cheeks, the jaw. Let your attention lightly scan this area just as a brush lightly touches a canvas. As you scan, relax the muscles so that your face is as soft and open as that of a sleeping baby. Continue to scan down the body, noting where there are knots of tension and releasing them as you go. Become aware of the sensations of the body, just noting them. Center on the sensation of the breath as it flows in and out. When thoughts arise, and they will, don't fight against them but try not to get carried away by them either. Just return your attention to your breath, in and out, in and out.

Stability comes with holding your body still and your mind quiet. Clarity brings a sense of brightness or aliveness to the process and is related to being aware of what you are doing. The ability to focus your attention with more ease and clarity is an added bonus of meditation. The greatest value will eventually come from becoming aware of your inner world and gaining some control over your own mind and actions.

When you meditate, you're conditioning the mind, training your mind for something. Traditionally in Asia, people didn't meditate just to reduce stress, although in the West it is a good place to start. Buddhists have a series of paradigm shifts that start with basic calm abiding and go on from there. If you've never meditated before, start small with following the breath practice. Begin with five minutes at a time, work up from there. 20 minutes a day can create wonders. In Buddhist countries like Bhutan, people go in and out of meditation all day rather than rope off 20 minutes in the morning. Once you've establish a meditation practice on the cushion you can (and should) fall into the practice of emptying and relaxing the mind throughout the day.

Meditation is easier to practice than to explain. We often have a lot of misconceptions about mediation that can get in the way. Tibetans say that it is a very natural thing, like drinking water. Also, it is something that you do every day, like drinking water.

So What Does Meditation Train The Mind To Do?

We are sick with a fascination for the useful tools of names and numbers, of symbols, signs, conceptions and ideas. Meditation is therefore the art of suspending verbal and symbolic thinking for a time, somewhat as a courteous audience will stop talking when a concert is about to begin.

~Alan Watts

We learn to focus, to pay attention.

Trains us to live in the present rather than the past or future.

Trains us to recognize impermanence. We begin to notice that just like our breath that comes and goes, our thoughts come and go, our emotions come and go, we come and go.

Trains us to watch our thoughts so that we become a witness to them rather than simply being controlled by them.

Allows us to create a gap between our thoughts, a space of openness in which we are awake and aware in a way that does not involve analytical thinking.

Both the gap and the witness allow us to become less reactive emotionally and more conscious of the reality of others.

As we begin to pay attention to others as subjects rather than as objects, once we see them as they are in their own ground, we begin to feel compassion for them.

The more we meditate, we less we are taken in by our fleeting, often deluded thoughts.

Teaches us to expand the gap and deepen into it by spending more time there.

The more our negative patterns of behavior dissolve, the more compassion arises spontaneously.

As we spend more time in nonverbal awareness, insights about the nature of mind begin to arise unexpectedly.

We discover deep mind.

MINDFULNESS

> For the ordinary mind, whose mind is a checkerboard of crisscrossing reflections, opinions, and prejudices, bare attention is virtually impossible; one's life is thus centered not on reality itself but in one's ideas about it.

~Philip Kapleau

The word "mindfulness" is today often used interchangeably with the term "meditation" or a code word for "stress reduction," but traditionally it has wider connotations, specifically in terms of becoming aware of cause and effect. Understanding that our own actions have real life consequences leads us to live a more ethical life.

Mindfulness includes paying attention to where you are paying that attention. As William James pointed out, whatever we attend to becomes our reality. We need to be able to track our minds rather than simply let them wander at will. At first, we must set our intention to do this, but in time it simply becomes second nature.

You are mindful of your breath in calm abiding meditation, you are mindful of your bodily sensations, such as tension in the face.

On and off the cushion, you can become mindful of your emotions, the workings of your mind, as well as your reactions to others and the effect of your actions on others and on yourself. You should also remain ever mindful of your motivation, your intentions and direction. Are you motivated solely by pleasure? How much of this pleasure depends on an outside source? Can you generate happiness from within yourself? Are you simply on a hedonic treadmill? What sort of person are you? Completely self-involved or helpful to others? Somewhere in between? Where are you headed in your life? What are your true aspirations and goals? Are your actions actually aligned with these goals? On the deepest level, what would you like to become? What would you like to contribute to the world? Looking back from age 84, what would you like to have accomplished?

Another thing to be mindful of is your own mind. Are you often distracted? Spaced out or dull? Do you live in reality? Fantasy? Day-dreams? Do you know how your mind works? Do you operate from concepts about how things should be rather than seeing how they actually are? How often do you fall into obsessive thinking? How do you get out of it? Can you stop the flow of your own thoughts? Are you high jacked by each thought as it goes by? Do you believe every-thing you think is 100% true just because you think it?

CONTEMPLATION

> Engaging in the three-stage process of study, contemplation, and meditation frees us to be ourselves.
>
> ~ Dzogchen Ponlop Rinpoche

Chagdud Tulku Rinpoche, raised in the old ways in Kham, Tibet, used to say that just to sit and meditate was like placing patches over the holes in your trousers when you sit. You stand up from the cushion and they fall off. He said that we needed to sew the patches on through teachings, study and contemplation. He went on to say that implementation through compassionate action was the final step of the process.

Today contemplation is often the most neglected part of dharma practice. We are going too fast, our world is too speedy. That's probably why our dharma trousers are still so full of holes, so to speak.

Contemplation or reflection means thoughtful concentration on a particular topic. The mind returns again and again to the topic without judging or rejecting it, but with openness toward understanding its true nature. We are contemplating when we fall into a "brown study" or when we let ourselves be spontaneously carried along by a flow of images and ideas as we stare into a fire.

Writing can serve as a form of contemplation if we retain an open attitude to the subject at hand. Often the act of the pen moving across the paper (or the fingers tapping a keyboard) grounds us as our mind gives itself over to contemplation.

BECOMING MORE EMOTIONALLY AWARE

Your emotions are the slaves to your thoughts, and you are the slave to your emotions.

~Elizabeth Gilbert,

It is a simple idea but a central one—emotions evolved to prepare us to deal quickly with the most vital events in our lives.

~Paul Ekman

Let's not forget that the little emotions are the great captains of our lives and we obey them without realizing it.

~Vincent Van Gogh, 1889

BACKGROUND NOTE

During the Mind and Life Conference on Destructive Emotions in 2000, HH the Dalai Lama listened to experts in the field of psychology as they described the emotional suffering common in the West. He pointed out that Buddhist practices already had a way to deal with most of these problems and requested that someone come up with a program that combined secular Buddhist techniques with Western psychological insights. This challenge was taken up by Dr. Paul Ekman, a pioneer in the study of emotions, and Dr. Alan Wallace, a noted meditation teacher. Between them they created a training program called "Cultivating Emotional Balance." I happened to be working as Alan Wallace's Program Director at the time, and helped to create the manual for this program and have since co-taught an off-shoot called "Cultivating Emotional Balance through Mindfulness," which grew out of the original training. The following chapter, "About Emotions," is based on Paul Ekman's work, especially his book *Emotions Revealed*. The rest of the section includes work from the courses that therapist Dr. Radhule Weininger (who attended the first CEB Teacher Training) and I have taught for the past four years as a six-week workshop series.

ABOUT EMOTIONS

Emotions are reactions to things that seem important to our welfare and often begin so quickly that we are not aware of what sets them off.

Emotions evolved to prepare us to be constantly (and unconsciously) on the lookout for important signals in the environment and to deal quickly with vital events in our lives. Emotions have a universal and a personal component. We automatically turn away in disgust from something that smells rotten, we automatically duck when something is thrown at us. These built in emotional responses have helped us to survive.

On a personal level, our experiences create a sort of psychological data base that we keep refining or adding to concerning what is going to protect us and to help us to survive on a physical and psychological level. Below the level of conscious awareness, we continually scan the environment to see what's coming at us. Driving along, not paying attention, another car comes towards us and without calculation, we hit the breaks or swerve.

Much of the time, for most people, our emotions serve us well, by mobilizing us to deal with what is most important in life and providing us with many different kinds of enjoyment. We get into trouble if we display too much or too little emotion or one that seems inappropriate.

Paul Ekman described seven basic emotional groups based on different facial expressions, all arising from an evolutionary utility:

Anger—readiness to fight; energy to remove obstacles. If a child is crawling across the floor and we interfere with his locomotion, he often becomes angry. Being thwarted is the basis for a response that ranges from mild irritation to rage.

Fear—flight, escape from danger; defensive, freeze in place.

Sadness—be reassured, elicit connection and caring from others, create connection in face of loss.

Happiness—deepens connection and co-operation.

Disgust—gets rid of something poisonous or harmful.

Surprise—focuses attention in order to identify something.

Contempt—asserts superiority either personally or within a group.

Therapists find other emotions that aren't necessarily tied to facial expressions (guilt, for instance), and poets would finely nuance the emotion of love, not just lump it in with happiness, but Ekman's work is an excellent place to start. He found that each group has its own distinctive physiology in terms of sweating, blood flow, and skin temperature. Anger, for instance, sends blood to the upper arms making them ready to strike out. With fear, blood flows to the legs, preparing for flight.

Emotions happen to us, usually very quickly. Charles Darwin made a small bet with a friend that he could put his face against the thick glass cage of a puff adder in the London Zoological Gardens and not move when the snake tried to strike. He lost. Without realizing he had even moved, he suddenly found himself several feet away from the striking snake. His mind might have been aware of the glass between them, but his emotions got him out of the way immediately, quick as a snake.

Each major emotional group has its own trigger. We each need to find out our own triggers for anger, fear, happiness, etc. and become intimately aware of our general emotional landscape—what emotions do you feel the most? Which do you avoid? Which emotions would you like to have more control over? Also, become mindful of the range of your emotions. How would you wish to expand this range?

Once you identify the specific triggers that set off each of the different emotions for you, try to become aware of the internal narrative that accompanies the trigger.

By creating scenes in our imagination that we know make us emotional, we can deconstruct their causes and more clearly understand their roots. Furthermore, we can, in our own minds or by writing it out, rehearse and imagine into other ways of interpreting what is occurring so that our usual hot triggers aren't so easily activated.

COGNITIVE FUSION

Memory, emotion, thoughts and reactions can become fused together so we react automatically to a situation on many levels, not realizing that the reaction comes from our emotional data base rather than the present situation. We can react just as strongly to a misperceived situation as to an actual one. If we suddenly come upon a coiled rope and take it for a snake, our fright is genuine. We need to realize that our emotional landscape is littered with coiled ropes.

Although emotions themselves can be of very short duration, we can replay them in our minds and they become stronger. The French psychiatrist, Hubert Benoit, calls this an emotive state which lasts much longer than the original emotion. Many studies have shown that emotions can be whipped up into a frenzy this second time around. Tibetans point out that it is as if someone shoots an arrow at us which falls to our feet, but then we pick up the arrow and stab ourselves over and over. Part of creating emotional balance is to feel the emotion as physical sensation without the emotive state, without linking it to the data base or our narrative about it. This also shortens what Ekman calls the "refractory period."

While in the refractory period, while we are in the grip of a strong emotion, we filter out information that contradicts this state, and focuses on whatever supports it. If we are in a fight and filled with intense feelings of anger, we literally can't remember anything we like or respect about the other person. Everything they say, we interpret to support our bad opinion of them. We can't take in any information that mediates the situation, our fixated minds are squeezed shut. This refractory period can last minutes or hours. Sometimes, it seems, days or months. We rarely have conscious control over this state, but through practice and meditation, we can learn to shorten it.

DEVELOPING EMOTIONAL AWARENESS

Two elements are especially important in developing emotional awareness. The first is to have a sense of our emotional history and how it impacts our emotional landscape today. The second is to keep an account of our current emotional episodes. Both involve writing, mindfulness, meditation, and active imagination.

Charting Your Emotional Landscape

When done in a group, this exercise takes about two hours, writing alternating with meditation in timed segments, separated by a bell. This process is repeated until all of the prompts are finished.

At home, you could set a kitchen timer or use one of the very handy timer applications made for tablets and smart phones. If it seems like too much writing, just jot down a number of key words.

PROMPTS:

Describe the room (s) you grew up in.

Did any one emotion dominate you in childhood?

What was the emotional tone of your family? What three words first come to mind?

What emotion of your mother's do you remember best? Your father's?

Did one parent or the other tend to emotionally dominate and control the home?

How did your siblings impact you growing up? Are you still in touch with them? How has your relationship with them changed? How stayed the same?

Remember a scene at the dinner table of your childhood home. Describe it in terms of interaction and communication.

In grade school, what was most important to you? How did you perceive yourself?

In high school what concerned you the most in school? Outside of class?

After school, what changed for you? Or what didn't change?

Recollect what it felt like to leave home and be on your own.

What of marriage? Describe your (first) mate and your early life together.

List your job history. Have you been happy with your working situations or profession? Have they brought you satisfaction?

What is the emotional tone of your current family? How this is similar to or different from your original family?

Where are you now?

Keeping an Emotional Episodes Notebook

For at least two weeks, keep a careful account of your emotional life: note your moods, your general outlook each day. Whenever an emotional episode occurs, describe it in some detail, as well the trigger, any physiological changes you noticed, and the refractory period. Was there an emotive state in which you chewed over the episode in detail? How long did it last? How were others affected by the episode? Imagine into how it could have ended differently.

Also check out the excellent free app that Dr.Radhule Weininger created for the CEBtM course: **www.mindfulpause.org**

EMOTIONAL MINDFULNESS

Become aware of your bodily sensations—not just of the breath—when meditating, but the physiological sensations in the body that accompany different emotions.

Become intimately aware of your general emotional landscape—what emotions do you feel the most? Which do you avoid?

Which emotions would you like to have more control over?

Be mindful of the range of your emotions. How would you wish to expand this range?

Be mindful of the specific triggers that set off each of the different emotions for you.

Be mindful of your own narrative about your life.

Watch how you respond emotionally to different people and situations. Too much? Too little? Inappropriately? Balanced except sometimes? Just right most of the time?

Become mindful of other people's emotions, how they are displayed, acted out.

Become mindful of pockets of resistance when different emotions arise. For example, which of these questions evoked a feeling of wanting to shove it away?

Become mindful of the effect of other people's emotions on you.

Become very mindful of the effect of your emotions on other people.

UNDERSTANDING THE STORY LINE

> We tell stories about who we are and what life is, but seldom see that they're only stories. The good news is that the truth is never far away. It's right here, in fact, posing as backdrop.
>
> ~Erik Hansen

A story line is what we add to events in our lives, the narrative by which we categorize and remember them. The story line can enhance the event in positive ways or can make it shiver with negativity. The story line is strung together by our ongoing commentary to ourselves, but it is based on real events.

The event: Susan went to the market this morning to buy an apple. It was a busy day and she waited in line to pay for it.

Susan's story line: "I went to market to buy an apple but had to wait forever in line. And did the clerk even bother to smile at me? No, not that one. She couldn't be bothered. I gave her a nice smile but she never even looked up. I'm the sort of person who always smiles at people. It makes them feel better. That stupid clerk could learn a lesson from me."

The phrase "I'm the sort of person who ...." is a dead giveaway that an embroidered story line is about to start.

Few things are as important to understand and become mindful of as our story line. Often an emotional trigger and story line are intimately related. We need to find out how our ongoing inner narrative shapes, fixates or expands our experience.

It isn't that the story line isn't true, often it can be quite factual. But it is partial. What else happened? What isn't included? What's being denied, rejected, covered over, ignored?

In the default mode, the story we tell ourselves about ourselves disappears and becomes a sort of background wallpaper to our lives, especially our emotional life. It is as if layers and layers of wallpaper have built up between us and the outside world. If we're lucky, we've been able to poke a few holes here and there, tear off a corner or enlarge a split, but the old layers are still there, blocking the view to the way things are.

ANGER

> For every moment you are angry, you lose sixty seconds of happiness.
>
> ~ Ralph Waldo Emerson

Anger is most dangerous of emotions because anger calls forth anger and can quickly escalate. Anger controls, punishes, retaliates. It has the potential to do long-term as well as short-term damage. Furthermore, when anger is happening, others things are crowded out. In anger there may be fear, but there is no love, no compassion, no empathy, no joy.

Anger ranges from mild irritation to violent rage. Everyone has his or her own trigger for anger and it is very helpful to locate yours. It may be in response to injustice or unfairness. Others are set off by disappointment in someone's actions. We expect them to act one way, they act another. We may respond with anger to being hurt or attacked, then either retreat or strike out against that which has made us angry. Someone else's anger is a common trigger.

There are tremendous differences in the way people experience anger. Some people just don't seem to get mad at all, while others go around looking for an excuse. With some, it is a form of foreplay, to others, so toxic they avoid it at all costs. Different cultures view anger in various ways: some admire it, others shun it.

What's good about anger? Often the same situation brings up both anger and fear. Anger can give us the surge to overcome fear and act more effectively. Anger also can provide tremendous energy. Restaurant kitchens, for instance, often run on rage, especially the chef. It gets the adrenaline pumping, the energy ramped up. Sometimes it has a sort of cleansing quality. It also provides signals to others—a glare means don't do that, don't say that, back off. It can also center energy and give us confidence in ourselves: I'm right, you're wrong. Being full of righteous indignation feels especially powerful and enjoyable in the refractory period. There's no confusion or middle ground, only this island of rightness that you inhabit. This feeling of being so very right can be a rush, but it prolongs the refractory period.

WRITING:

Think back to a time when you were angry. What type is your anger? Hot? Cold? Hard and defensive? Write about its effects on you. On another person.

Describe an event when one of the above types of anger was directed at you. How did it make you feel? How did you react? How is this type of anger different from or similar to your own?

What other types of anger have you experienced in yourself or coming from others? Describe an event in which this type of anger dominated.

Remember an angry incident. Frown and glare to recreate the emotion. What does it feel like? Are other emotions involved? Describe the incident in detail.

What triggered this anger? Is this a typical trigger? Contemplate your trigger, uncover its origins, recollect its history.

Remember an angry encounter with another person. Write about the event from the other person's point of view.

Does anger serve a useful purpose in your life?

Describe what you like about anger.

If your anger were an animal, what animal would it be? Wolverine? Barking Chihuahua? Pit bull? Snake? Swarm of black gnats? Domestic cat? Saber tooth tiger? Diving bird? Retreating mouse? Is your animal the same one when relating to your mother as it is to others? Your father? Your partner or spouse? Your friends? Maybe you have an array of animals. A whole zoo. What sounds do these animals make? How do they act in different situations?

What part did anger play in your life as a child? Describe the role of anger as you experienced it yourself and coming from others.

Remember an angry encounter. Indentify a point where it could have gone another way. Describe a different ending.

Remember an incident which involved anger. What is the story line that has grown up around this incident? Examine it closely.

Remember an incident which involved anger. Try to experience the emotion without the storyline. Describe the result.

Make a list of incidents involving anger that ended badly.

Make another list of incidents involving anger that ended well. Compare these lists.

FEAR

> Fear demands to be felt, and it can be felt most readily
> in the body, as a powerful sensation. The experience
> may be uncomfortable, but as you watch fear man-
> ifest in the body, the truth of the Buddha's words is
> revealed: It does arise because of conditions. It is not
> a wall of emotion, but a constantly changing process.
> And it finally ends. It has its say and departs.
>
> ~David Guy

Fear is often part of other emotions as well as standing alone. We
need to know what triggers our fears, how it effects us physiological-
ly, and also the strategies we've worked up to deal with it. The most
talked about reactions are flight or fight, but there are many varia-
tions within these two.

Ask yourself: is this fear based on facts or am I manufacturing some
future disaster? On a trip, I'm afraid I'm not going to get to the airport on time. Got to the airport fine, now I'm afraid that the flight is
going to be late and I'll miss my connection. I made the connection,
now I'm afraid that they've lost my luggage....

A certain type of fear is almost always about the next thing. The feeling of anxiety is real, but the reasons our minds create around it are
conjuring up the worst case scenario.

As in the above case, the thoughts are not true, but the feeling itself
is real. Be with the feeling as sensation, separate it from your narrative about it, see that the expectation may not be true. Creating a
narrative gives us something to do with the emotion. Fear can create
a sort of mental spinning top that distances us from the feeling itself
as we imagine what can go wrong – often very creatively. But this
response can become a habit that limits us, robs us of the present
moment.

We don't want to give up fear. Think of it as a warning system that
we need. If we can't swim, then we should be afraid of water. When
we feel panicky, it's a sign that we are going over our own speed limit.

Fear often fuels speediness. It's a signal that we need to calm down.

WRITE the word 'fear' in the middle of the page. Free associate and jot down whatever comes to mind. Explore three of these jottings in more detail.

Make a list of the things that you currently fear. Make another list of things that you feared in the past but fear no longer. What do they hold in common?

How much of your fear lies in the future? Make a list of things you have been afraid of that never happened.

Fear is meant to protect you. Describe the ways in which a fear does its job well.

Describe the ways in which being afraid limits your life. What would happen if you gave up these fears?

How much of your mental activity is taken up with fearful thoughts? What is the story line connected with these fears? Feel the emotion without the story line.

Write for ten minutes from a fearless point of view.

Recreate a situation in which you were afraid. Try to feel the fear fully and to recreate its emotional intensity. Turn it into a poem.

Describe a chronic fear and the effect it has had on your life. Give the fear a name and enter into a dialogue with it.

Visualize your fears—large and small—see them as animals, insects, funny looking creatures from the deep. Get to know them, befriend them, feed them, and let them go.

List five ways in which you deal with fear or have dealt with it in the past. Star the ones that seemed the most effective. Put an X by the ones than never work.

Take 20 deep breaths as you visualize your fears, then write for 20 minutes without stopping on whatever comes into your mind.

Sit in a chair, facing an empty one. Visualize a specific fear in the chair opposite. Give it a face, a name. Ask this fear what it wants. What it needs. Change places and, as the visualized fear, answer these questions. For more on this technique see Tsultrim Allione's Feeding Your Demons.

Meditation/Contemplation: visualize a small fear in your life. Spiders, parking, interacting with certain people. Bring it to mind vividly, then back away from the narrative and sink into the feeling; feel the fear, don't back away from it, just feel it as a sensation. You're safe, this is remembered fear. Now go into the narrative, into the story line. Is it true? What would happened if you didn't have this story line?

THE HUT OF HOPE AND FEAR

> I don't like hope very much. In fact, I hate it. It's the crystal meth of emotions. It hooks you fast and kills you hard. It's bad news. The worst. It's sharp sticks and cherry bombs. When hope shows up, it's only a matter of time until someone gets hurt.
>
> ~ Jennifer Donnelly

A Tibetan teacher used to say that we lived in a hut that we'd built up out of hope and fear. "Tear down hut," he'd say in his funny English. "See sky."

Hope and fear are often flip sides of the same coin: we hope this will happen, we are afraid that it won't. We hope he loves us, but are afraid that he doesn't. You get the idea.

Being ever hopeful is often seen as positive, as a stance we need to take and stay rooted there in the face of all comers. But hope, too, can keep us from what is. We hope we're not going to die, but of course we die anyway. We hope that we or our loved ones will not get sick, but it is built into the system. Hope and denial are good friends and work together to keep at bay things as they are.

CONTEMPLATE: What sort of dwellings have you built out of hope and fear?

A confining hut created from fear and doubt? Are you huddled there, unable to see the vast expanse of sky?

Or is it a fortress where nothing negative is ever allowed to enter?

Examine the foundation, the permeability of the walls. Does it have to be protected at all times to maintain its positive aspects? How much energy goes into keeping out the shadow? What else could you be doing with that energy?

In either case, you've hired a contractor to align your dwelling with reality. Where does he start? What changes?

GRIEF

> When someone you love dies, you have a feeling of numbness; a yearning; and a protest. You have lost part of yourself; you feel disorganized; and you do much crying. You're restless, and you may feel guilty. Perhaps you could have helped the one who died but you did not know how. You are angry because the person died, and you are angry at the world. You feel so alone, and loneliness is one of the biggest problems of grief. It is your problem and you have to solve it alone.
>
> ~ Elizabeth KublerRoss

When my beloved husband of thirty years died, I understood grief for the first time. Nothing anyone had ever written had prepared me for its reality. Nothing I can write now will prepare you. It's a journey and landscape of its own, a sort of alternate reality that is unimagined and unimaginable until experienced.

Writing does help, although perhaps not at first, but as time passes. But this, like every other aspect of the experience, is different for each individual. Make the grief your own and honor the process.

1. Write about the death of a loved one. Write in the third person if you wish.

2. Write about loss: start before you experienced the loss, appreciate what you had, then write about how the loss occurred, and what changes the absence has created in your life. Take your time.

3. Make a list of things that you fear you will lose. Contemplate how the loss might impact your life. Appreciate the fact that they are still with you.

JOY AND HAPPINESS

Neuroscientists tell us that during evolution our brains have learned to look out for that which might harm us. If two men were standing on a plain during the Ice Age, the one who noted the danger of an approaching woolly mammoth and ran away would be more likely to survive than the other who stands there lost in contemplating the beauty of a sunset. Apparently this translates into an inclination toward the negative in terms of the psychological woolly mammoths our brains see charging toward us today. And it's true that at the end of the day we seem to grind over what has been upsetting rather than what has brought us happiness. Thanks to neuroplasticity, the ability of the brain to rewire itself, we can begin to reverse this unfortunate mental pattern by consciously dwelling on the positive and spending more time deeply experiencing that which bring us joy and happiness. Writing and/or contemplating allow us to do just that.

Take a Happiness Break: remember a happy event in your life. Dwell on it, milk it for emotion. Stay with the good feeling. If that starts to feel contrived, go on to another.

Watch a baby, or go to YouTube and search for babies laughing (there are several). Listen to a clip over and over until you begin to feel a little frisson of joy around the heart area.

For more on neuroplasticity and how to rewire our brains, see Rick Hanson's *Buddha's Brain: the practical neuroscience of happiness, love and wisdom* and Sharon Begley's *Train Your Mind, Change Your Brain.*

BLESSINGS JOURNAL

> When we give cheerfully and accept gratefully,
> everyone is blessed.
>
> ~Maya Angelou

A Blessings Journal is an ongoing record of whatever makes you feel blessed. It also helps to rewire the brain toward the positive. Write in it when you experience a spontaneous surge of gratitude—for a hummingbird that comes to your window, the way the light filters though a slatted blind, the smile of a passing child. Read it when you feel depressed.

Start a journal of things you'd like to do for other people to make them happy.

Commit random acts of kindness.

Each day remember three things that made you happy.

Each day remember three things you did for someone else that made them happy.

OPPOSITES JOURNAL

In *A Life Of One's Own*, Joanna Field writes that she started keeping what she called "An Opposites Journal" to try to maintain her life in balance. She noticed early on that for every strong opinion she had, she often held (or was capable of entertaining) its opposite. Also, periods of great happiness and deep despair punctuated her life, but when she was in one she couldn't remember the other until she sat down to write about it in her "opposites journal." This kind of journal is extremely valuable for breaking through dualistic or polarized thinking, especially if you mark some of the pages in columns so that you can list opposing thoughts side by side. Good Traits - Bad Traits, etc.

LOVE

> The problem with interpersonal love is that you are dependent on the other person to reflect love back to you. That's part of the illusion of separateness. The reality is that love is a state of being that comes from within.
>
> ~ Ram Dass

Love is that which connects, it is heart based, not always verbal, but a feeling in the body, in the heart. The language of the heart is softer and quieter than the language of the mind. Too often the mind dominates and cuts us off from love.

There are many different ways that love manifests, ranging from transpersonal and unconditional all the way through to grasping and self-serving.

Let's start at the beginning:

Buddhist say that when the sperm and the ovum unite, a spark is born. That spark is unsullied, immutable, doesn't change. It is a tiny seed within all sentient beings, born of ecstasy. Buddhists call it Buddha Nature, Christians call it God within or Christ Consciousness, others have different names. Whatever it is called, it is there. A great deal of the spiritual path involves finding our way back to it. We can feel its pull, a subtle longing of the heart to reconnect.

The Buddhists go on to say that this spark has three main elements: openness (sometimes translated as spaciousness or emptiness, in that it is empty of your projections and preconceptions). The second element is clarity or awareness: the ability to turn inward and understand and guide the nature of our own minds. The third can be called essence love, a sort of unconditional kindness or innate compassion.

Tsoknyi Rinpoche, in *Open Heart Open Mind* describes it this way:

> Essence love, like emptiness and clarity, stands beyond all the names we call ourselves and the roles we play in life: son, daughter, father, mother, husband, wife, and so on. It's not something manufactured, nor can it be destroyed, because it emerges spon-

taneously from the inseparability of emptiness and clarity, which are themselves uncreated. It may best be described as a very basic sense of well-being, which, if nurtured properly, can extend to a kinship with all other living beings. As Albert Einstein once wrote to a friend, 'A human being is a part of a whole called by us the universe.'

Every Buddhist meditation practice ultimately turns toward a reconnection with essence love.

Essence love is part of deep mind, transpersonal and below our normal range of consciousness. As it moves into the world of form, as it surges into individual waves, it reveals itself in different ways:

As it meets with pain, essence love becomes compassion.

As it meets with irritation or anger, it becomes patience.

As it meets with poverty or need, it becomes generosity.

As it meets with confusion, it becomes clarity/attention.

It spontaneously seeks to heal, to help, to make whole.

However, once it gets caught up in the world of dualism, of ego, it can become distorted, a commodity that is traded back and forth. When the generalized essence love becomes "I Love You" it is bracketed in by subject and object, entangled with hope and fear, with anger and revenge. This causes both much happiness and much grief plus, of course, leads to more sparks being born through the sperm and ovum uniting.

To get back to essence love, to return to deep mind, leaving the choppy waves of I and Other behind, we need to meditate.

MEDITATION: Essence Love

To experience a taste of essence love, close your eyes, take a deep breath, and relax completely. Recreate a sense of what makes you feel deeply happy and connected with the world. Don't think about it, just feel it in the body, the heart.

When you feel some small spark of general well-being, a sense of warmth, gently connect with it. Don't pounce on it, don't try to do anything with it, just feel it. That is a taste of essence love. It may be accompanied by a feeling of joy, but not one that is dependent on an external cause, but joy that arises spontaneously. It may seem dim and far away, but will grow stronger as you connect with that part of yourself that is warm and content.

Just touch it lightly with your awareness, then let it go. If you try to grab onto it, it becomes frozen as we fixate on it. Just brush against that feeling of well-being again and again, letting go each time. Opening up space around the feeling makes the connection stronger, letting it become a part of our everyday life.

WRITING ABOUT LOVE

Exercise One:

Use the technique of "clustering" to find out what you think about a subject: Write the word "love" in the middle of a sheet of paper and free associate. Write down whatever words or phrases come to mind. Keep going way beyond a politically correct idea about love. Contemplate what you have written.

Don't think, write.

Exercise Two:

Enter into a dialogue with love. Begin with:

I said to love:

Love said to me:

Then continue the dialogue for at least five minutes:

Me:

Love:

Me:

Love:

Surprise yourself.

Without self-judgment examine where you have imposed limits on loving or feeling love. Where have love and fear become entangled? Explore who or what you are trying to protect and see if it is really needed.

Bring to mind a difficult situation in your life. Ask yourself: What would love do now?

AYYA KHEMA ON LOVE

In all developed societies there are institutions to foster the expansion of the mind, from the age of three until death. But we don't have any institutions to develop the heart, so we have to do it ourselves. Most people are either waiting for or relating to the one person who makes it possible for them to feel love at last. But that kind of love is beset with fear, and fear is part of hate. What we hate is the idea that this special person may die, walk away, have other feelings and thoughts—in other words, the fear that love may end, because we believe that love is situated strictly in that one person. Since there are six billion people on this planet, this is rather absurd. Yet most people think that our love-ability is dependent upon one person and having that one person near us. That creates the fear of loss, and love beset by fear cannot be pure. We create a dependency upon that person, and on his or her ideas and emotions. There is no freedom in that, no freedom to love.

Imagine a day in the future when you have decided to simply love everyone you meet. Describe it. Try this at home.

How has love has played out in your life. Given? Received? Denied? Never enough? Too much? Enjoyed? Sustained by? Grasped onto? Thrown away? Diverted? Wished for? Fantasized about? Snatched away? Misinterpreted? Rejected? Feared? Flowing naturally? Embodied? Prime motivator? A little of everything?

COMPASSION

Compassion is the basis of morality.

~Arthur Schopenhauer

Through mindfulness, meditation, and contemplation we discover the causes of suffering and through developing focus, stability, clarity and loving kindness we develop an open heart and that brings an end to suffering for ourselves. But then, when we look around and see that others are still suffering, a spontaneous desire arises to help them.

Every human being has the same potential for compassion; the only question is whether we really take any care to create circumstances that allow it to develop, and then—very important—implement it in our daily life. This can be difficult, but we can't just believe in compassion, we have to live it.

We don't live in a compassionate age, but what is called the Kali Yuga, the age of strife, discord, quarrel, or contention. Also the age of spiritual degeneration and false teachers. Our culture doesn't stress compassion, in fact, our economic system tramples all over it. Our educational system pays more attention to self-esteem than to cultivating or implementing compassion. So we have to make an authentic effort ourselves.

We need to avoid something called "idiot compassion" where we fake up a sort of goopy concern for every little thing: For you to say "Oh, it's raining, the poor little birdies are getting wet. I'll go out and put up my umbrella over the birdbath" is more about you as a "compassionate" person than it is about the birds. This sort of faux compassion might produce a gushy feeling of being good, but again, this is all about you. Your actions have to _be_ compassionate without drawing attention to yourself. In this sense, compassion is a state of being rather than an emotion you feel. As Thich Nhat Hanh puts it: "Compassion is a verb."

The classic definition of compassion is wanting others to be free from suffering. The Buddhist view is that to generate genuine compassion, one needs to realize that an end to suffering is possible, furthermore, all beings suffer, and they also want to be free from suffering.

The question is: what are we suffering from?

Basically we suffer because we feel we don't have enough options. We don't want to get old, that's not an option, we don't want to get sick, not an option, we certainly don't want to die, but everyone does. We don't want things to change. Well, look around you. So we are at odds with the reality of being human and that is one type of suffering.

It's been said that a quarter of our suffering comes from uncontrollable events and three quarters from trying to avoid the first quarter. Lots of truth in that.

Buddha says that we suffer because of attachment or craving.

How   can   attachment   bring   us   suffering?

Let's take a look at the way people used to catch monkeys in South India:

One takes a coconut and makes a hole in it, just large enough so a monkey can squeeze its hand in. Tie the coconut down, and put a sweet inside. What happens next is pure attachment. The monkey smells the sweet, puts his hand into the coconut, grabs the sweet but finds that the hole is too small to release his fist from the coconut. The last thing a monkey would consider is to let go of the sweet, so it is literally tied down by its own attachment. Often they only let go when they fall asleep or become unconscious because of exhaustion.

The monkey is clinging to sweets. *What are we grasping onto?*

Often what we clench in our own fist is a false view of reality, of ourselves, of the world and our place in it.

It is here that Western culture and Buddhism come together.

In the Greek myth of the very handsome Narcissus, he sees his own image in the water, falls in love with it, becomes fixated on it and ultimately tumbles in and drowns.

He doesn't fall in love with himself, but with a reflected image of himself. Buddhists call this self-cherishing or ego-clinging. but it comes to the same thing.

Contemplate the things in your life that cause you to suffer. What is central to all of them?

EXPANDING OUR EMOTIONAL RANGE

In addition to love and compassion, those heavy hitters of positive emotions, several others come to mind:

Generosity

Remember gifts that you've given or been given. Think of times when someone was generous with their time, their attention.

Make a list of "random acts of kindness" you'd like to perform for others. Start with those you love, move on to your neighbors, people passing by, strangers.

The next time someone talks to you, really listen. Don't interrupt to tell them what a good listener you are, just pay deep attention to what they are saying.

Gratitude

On a day that has nothing to do with turkey or cranberry sauce, look around and count your many blessings. Not the obvious ones, but things you might tend to take for granted like electricity and indoor plumbing. Keep looking. Examine your body. No matter what the size or shape or condition, it's pretty miraculous: those opposable thumbs, inner ear balance, a pumping heart.

Empathy

You can come to truly understand other people through writing about them. Start with a physical description of someone you know well, then tell their history. Where did they come from? What were their greatest challenges? Their biggest triumphs? Their turning points? Write about their personality. How are they different from other people? What makes them unique? What are their relationships like with other people? What makes them happy? Sad? Experience their suffering. What is their life like day by day? Imagine yourself as that person and write about your day. Write about yourself from their point of view. Become that person, walk in their shoes.

Joy

A joyful mind is one of life's greatest blessings. If you weren't fortunate enough to have been born innately joyful, now's the time to start helping things along.

Often joy pops up spontaneously whereas happiness is frequently dependent on an outside stimulus. We are "surprised into joy" when we enter into the present moment that is not crowded with our agendas and concepts. We may seek for happiness outside, but for joy we must create space for it to arise spontaneously.

Notice scenes of joy throughout the day that have nothing to do with you: a happy dog, lovers entwined, mothers with their children. Empathetically experience their joy.

ALL PURPOSE ADVICE
FOR WRITERS

What is the most common advice to aspiring writers? "Write what you know." Write about your own life, disguised so that you don't get sued. Write about the world that is actually around you -- you in specific. Write the details and the moods of your own experience. Wise advice if you want to play safe. It is an insidious mediocretizing influence on today's literature. Especially in a world in which everyone, everyone is steeped in the same information culture, in which everyone knows the same base material, the dictum to write what you know leads to a rather bland commercialism. Writing, at least some of the time for some people, should to be an act of imagination, a magnificent risk, a reach outside of what you know. To tell an ambitious young writer to narrate what she knows is like telling a young sprinter with Olympian dreams, "Hey Dude, walking is easier." It is. You are less likely to fall and break something. But the few people who actually bother to run are going to beat you. If you're a writer, your most difficult challenge and most important asset is your imagination.

~ Michael S. A. Graziano

PLANNING TO WRITE

> For me, writing is the only thing that passes the three tests
> of métier: (1) when I'm doing it, I don't feel that I should
> be doing something else instead; (2) it produces a sense
> of accomplishment, and, once in a while, pride; and (3) it's
> frightening.
>
> ~Gloria Steinem

First, set your intention on what you want to write about rather than
the finished product. Decide how long you want to spend on this
project each day. Dialogue with yourself. Say, "Self, we need to talk. I
know we are busy, but let's make a commitment to write on this particular project for, say, a month. That's all. One month. Okay, self?
You with me on this?"

Start small. 15 minutes is better than an hour. You can always go
longer. Start with this sentence, this paragraph, this chapter. Con-
centrate on just writing, not on the trilogy you plan to write or what
you are going to wear on the book tour. If you create an ambitious
schedule requiring how much you think you should or could write
every day, it can be a setup for failure.

WRITING

> I started writing because of terrible feeling of power-
> lessness: I felt I was drifting and obscure, and I rebelled
> against that. I didn't see what I could do to change my
> condition. I wanted to control rather than be controlled,
> to ordain rather than be ordained, to relegate rather than
> be relegated.
>
> ~Anita Brookner

If you are working on a computer, date and file stamp everything.
You can do so in Word by going to insert/autotext/header/footer.
That way you can find things later.

Read as much as possible. Start watching for techniques, methods.
Learn to read on a craftsman level.

Warm up before you start your project. Pre-write in a notebook or
journal then ease your way into your writing project.

Write it out, edit it down later. Don't try to edit as you go along.

Think like a poet. Find metaphors. Interesting language, concise way
of saying things. Get outside the box.

Take advantage of the "find and replace" function on your computer. Change names, genders, locations. .

 Experiment with different genres. If you are having trouble writing
dialogue, write a play or turn parts of your fiction into a play. Works
every time.

Be curious about others, about the world.

Expect delays, bad days and flat spots.

Understand that suffering is built into the writing life as it is everywhere else. Accept it with grace.

EDITING AND REVISION

There is no great writing, only great rewriting.

~Louis Brandeis

Let a manuscript sit as long as you can before going back to it. Then, as much as possible, let go of your attachment to it, and treat it as an object to be shaped and improved.

Visualize your audience.

Just because you like the way you said something doesn't mean that it belongs in a particular passage. Cut and paste the part you like into an ongoing file called KEEP and use it elsewhere.

Be grateful to those who are willing to read your words. Don't argue with them or defend your choices. Thank them.

Only use feedback that is useful. Often someone will spot a problem and offer a solution. Feel free to ignore their solutions, but investigate the problem seriously.

Learn to go deeper and to flesh out passages during the rewrite. For instance, this rewrite from my novel *It Changes*:

Original:

After Leo told Helen he didn't want to get married, there followed a surreal period in which Helen pretended never to be able to hear his protests, but pulled every trick in the feminine arsenal. Her most maddening ploy was to convert whatever he said into its opposite. Leo was at his wit's end.

Expanded:

After Leo told Helen he didn't want to get married, there followed a surreal period in which Helen pretended never to be able to hear his protests.

"I think teal for the bridesmaids' dresses, don't you Hon?" she might say.

"What wedding are you talking about, Helen?"

"Though if you'd rather have blue, that's okay. But blue does make me look sallow."

"I think we have a little problem in communication here. There isn't going to be a wedding, Helen. Not for us."

"Well, don't use that tone of voice, Leo. You know how it hurts my feelings when you get angry." She'd begin to sniff threateningly.

Leo would react instinctively to the rising hysteria in her voice. "Don't start, okay?"

Blinking back her tears, she'd begin to smile coyly, then start to work on his buttons.

Even in the smallest ways she'd convert whatever he said into its opposite. There was a certain wonderful madness about it, as if her plan was to somehow reverse the way he processed information, to re-educate him so if she said black, he'd see white. He'd declare he didn't want to go out for a walk, only to find her waiting by the door, his coat thoughtfully over her arm. Or he might tell her after dinner, "No, I don't think I want any coffee, but a cup of tea would be nice." Only minutes later she'd be holding out a brimming cup of French Roast for him.

"Hope it doesn't keep you from sleeping," she'd murmur solicitously.

Leo was at his wit's end. What could he do, simply walk out the door? He could hear Savannah's little snort of laughter: "Leo! What a brilliant thought."

The trick is to slow down with the scene, sink into it, give it time and space to unfold naturally. Stop and follow your breath for a few minutes, then go back to writing.

ON HAVING WRITTEN

Don't show your work too soon.

Don't talk about your work too often. This dissipates energy and bores others.

Be careful to whom you show your work. Better a paid editor who knows what he or she is doing than a family member who has an agenda.

Join a writing group if you can find the right one.

Finding an agent can sometimes be a difficult, humiliating, time-consuming, thankless process that comes to nothing. Remember that this has little to do with the quality of your work.

If you can't find an agent (and even published authors have problems doing so), you might try approaching a press directly. This tends to work best with small presses.

Remember that the more you write, the better you get.

Trust only 50 % of what your agent/publisher tells you. Less if they are in Hollywood.

Don't expect applause.

Keep going.

PROMPTS FOR OVERCOMING THE FEAR OF WRITING.

> Blank pages inspire me with terror.
>
> ~Margaret Atwood

If you are afraid of writing—and many people are—these exercises may help to lessen anxiety.

1. Visualize and describe a private place where you feel safe to write. It may be anywhere—your real writing room, a spot outdoors, somewhere in another dimension. Visualize it in detail. Return to this place each time you begin to write.

At least at first, you might imagine bars on the windows to keep out every English teacher you've ever had. Nobody can see what you write or how you write in this space.

2. Imagine yourself as a kindly, compassionate editor or teacher and give yourself advice on writing.

3. Doodle all over the page.

4. Visualize your fear of writing: a teacher with fangs, a professor with a whip, yourself with a copy of Henry James, etc. Give them names and ask them their origins. Talk to these fears. Find out what they want. Politely show them to the door and lock it behind them.

5. Ask yourself: "Who is it that is afraid?" Then ask: "Who is writing?"

6. Try to locate the fear in your mind. Where does it come from, where does it dwell, where does it go when it leaves? Feel the fear in your body. Stay still and experience the fear simply as sensation without attaching a story line to it. What happens?

7. Remember a peaceful scene after you sit down at your desk. Visualize yourself as your favorite writer. Pick up your pen and begin.

8. Take 20 deep breaths before you start to write.

9. Meditate for a few minutes, following your breath. Keep doing so as you write, with part of your attention still on your breathing.

10. Find photos of people or animals who look fearless. Gaze at them often as you write.

FORMING A WRITING GROUP

A writing group or workshop can be very useful in providing deadlines, feedback, and a sense of not being alone. You can join a workshop simply for the pleasure of getting together with others to share ideas and writings. Or you can let the workshop function as a sort of way-station towards publication: a place where you present a piece to a small, knowledgeable (usually sympathetic) circle, then refine and rewrite it before going public. Or both.

If you want to start a workshop in a new locale, put a notice in the newspaper or on the bulletin board of your favorite local restaurant, yoga studio, bookstore, or wherever you see people you want to get to know better. Suggest a time and place to meet, then let the group decide on the ongoing structure in the first meeting. Some pre-planning can be decided by e-mail or phone.

The exercises from this book or various online sites provide a quick way for a group to get started, assuming that not everyone has a work in progress. During the first meeting, you may want to write as a group, then share your work. On subsequent meetings, bring in enough copies for everyone of exercises or other work completed at home. Let these exercises evolve into stories, poems or essays which you continue to rewrite and refine in light of the group's feedback. It helps to keep a workshop small (about three to five working members is plenty). A larger group, especially if each member writes a great deal, creates the problem of covering everyone's work in any sort of depth. How often you meet depends on you. Some groups meet weekly for six weeks, then never again. Others have been meeting once a month for years. The group that I'm in used to meet once a month, but now meets only when someone finishes a project and wants feedback on it. In general, all workshops are defined by time available, work produced, and the quality of the group's interaction.

Before asking a new member to join a group, it is a good idea to have this writer come as a guest for several meetings. Try to find writers who are at about the same level of expertise and ambition. Avoid people who are highly defensive, excessively negative, or narcissistic.

The writing workshops that I've been in work this way: each member brings in a portion of a work in progress, hands out Xeroxed copies to the group, then reads aloud. The members of the group then "workshop" the piece: How does it function as a whole? Do all the parts fit together? How can it be improved? Is the voice right? Is it clear? What succeeds best in the piece? What are its strengths? An honest but non-judgmental approach is always best when giving critiques in a workshop setting.

Special Focus Writing Groups

The focus in your workshop may not be on the writing itself at all, but a specific topic agreed upon by the group such as cancer, addiction, grief. Shared religious beliefs lend themselves to writing groups as well. In these groups, writing is used as a springboard for discussion, a way to get at difficult or partly understood material and going deeper. Generally, writing together and/or sharing what you've written creates a unique atmosphere. Meditating before you begin to write adds a deeper dimension to the process. Offering your own words to others and responding to theirs is a form of generosity that can create a common bond as well as an appreciation of another's methods and techniques.

Online Writing Groups

Since everyone these days stays so busy, sometimes an e-mail workshop is better than a face-to-face one. This is especially true if the e-mail group is combined with an occasional meeting. Simply make an e-mail list on your mail program, putting everyone's e-mail into a single list. When someone gets a message, they press RESPOND TO ALL, thus everyone on the list receives the same e-mail. Be sure to include yourself in your list. When people in the workshop finish a story or a non-fiction piece, they send it as an e-mail attachment to those on the list. It might be helpful to set up guidelines in the beginning. Set a date—say May 1st to June 1st—when people will submit their stories. Then decide another set of dates for feedback— say June 1st to June 15th. It may be helpful to arrange a face-to-face meeting sometime after that. Then repeat the cycle over again, maybe once a quarter or once every two months, depending on the group.

Guidelines For Offering Feedback

<u>Authors:</u>

Authors remain quiet while the other workshop participants give feedback. Listening to others' responses to our work is often more valuable than directing their conversation. As author, you might want to take notes or record comments on your cell phone during the workshop so that you can later refer to the discussion at home.

<u>Responders:</u>

If you are the first to respond, remember to begin with something that the author did well. Then elicit feedback on what was confusing and/or what the author might improve. "I liked this very much" may be polite, but is not considered a helpful comment in a workshop. Be as specific as you possibly can if you are providing feedback.

Keep your responses brief so others will have a chance to speak. You may need to assign a moderator who reserves the right to interrupt others who are speaking inappropriately or are speaking for too long. It is best not to interrupt each other. Sometimes passing around an object such as a "talking stick" will help to keep things on track.

The intent of respectful readers is to try to determine the author's intentions and help her/him achieve those goals—not to rewrite the essay according to our own preferences or desires, and not to psychoanalyze the author or to criticize or comment on their life choices. It is helpful to keep this in mind when giving comments. The moderator may step in quickly if she feels that someone is crossing the line into psychoanalysis during the commentary period. This is to protect authors, not to discipline responders.

Direct your comments to the group as a whole, not just to the author or the instructor.

When discussing the narrator of a text, refer to that individual as "the narrator" or "the main character" not as "you." This creates a necessary gap between the author and the work itself.

Writing in a group can be a powerful experience, especially when it is connected with meditation. It might be a good idea to meditate together before writing together, and factor in social time toward the end of the meeting. Just saying.

To get the group started, you might pick an exercise from this book and write for 20 minutes. Share your writing and insights with the group. Eventually you'll find your own writing topics or share work in progress.

Resources:

Judith Barrington, *Writing the Memoir*, 2002

Maureen Murdock, *Unreliable Truth: On Memoir and Memory*, 2003

William Zinsser, *Inventing the Turth: The Art and Craft of Memoir* 1998

JOURNALING

THE SELF

&

THE STORY LINE

To study the way is to study the self; to study the self is to forget the self.

To forget the self is to be enlightened by the world's myriad things.

~Dogen

To really study yourself is not to study the monkey-mind surface mind but to drop down into a deeper level. This is just me whether I'm recognized or criticized I'm just me. I'm unique and special in this lifetime only.

~Roshi Pat Enkyo O'Hara

JOURNALING

Journals and personal writing can often be our best friends, keeping us company on our day to day journey and sustaining us when things fall apart. Like calm abiding meditation, journaling helps to ground and orient us, stabilize our emotions and clarify our scattered thoughts.

Journals can also be invaluable as source material for waking up to things as they are. Go back and read your journals, looking for the underlying narrative, the tone of voice, hints as to your deeper patterns, good and bad. Where are the battlegrounds? The defensive barricades? Have they changed over the years? Growth is recorded there as well, acts of kindness and generosity. Hopes and fears. Often it is all there in your journals, caught in the raw moment as events occurred, before they were photoshopped by memory.

Take heart and look back through them. Breathe.

From Journal to Memoir and Back Again

> People write memoir for many reasons. Some write to discover their old story, to recover what was lost, to touch it once again, to put it on record. Others use memoir to find the true self—hidden beneath public persona of ambition, success, heartache or failure. Still others write to bear witness to their life –I lived, I loved, I experienced loss and I yearned just like you. Some writers explore memoir to lay the family demons to rest, to let them go once and for all, so that they may fully live their present "story." Others write memoir to heal a relationship, to come to terms with an illness, to find community. But more often than not, people write memoir because their story just must be told.
>
> ~ Maureen Murdock, *Unreliable Truth: On Memoir and Memory*

Many, if not most, memoirs grow out of material first written in a journal. In some cases, long passages may be identical and the specific content exactly the same. The major difference can be summed up in a single word: audience.

It is doubtful that anyone who is immersed in the creative flow is writing with an audience in mind. This comes in later, with the editing, the reworking, the rewriting. During this secondary process, what's been produced within the timeless world of the imagination is by necessity turned into an object that needs to be shaped into a particular genre or form. Since memoir is very close to the personal history recorded in a journal, we often resist changing it at all. "But it didn't happen exactly that way," can be the response. But, like other genres, memoir needs to be reworked for an audience.

Traditionally, a memoir focuses on a single-strand of one's life, sometimes concentrating on a particular time or place ("My Years in the White House") or on a specific activity ("My Life as a Chef"). Although a memoir is based on truth, it usually incorporates elements of fiction. Often characters are conflated, names changed, and events rearranged in order to make the work more comprehensible and readable. "Lie in order to be more true," as Henry Miller put it.

Rather than simply relating that first this happened, then that, the memoirist has an audience to entertain, to enlighten. Details that may seem boring or irrelevant to the reader must be cast aside. As a memoirist you must both tell the story and muse about it, attempting to unravel what it means to you at this stage in your life. And, as if that weren't enough, you have to get at the emotional truth of these events that are often hidden behind your sometimes faulty memory.

Somewhere in this process, you may lose a sense of the original experience itself. For instance, early in my career as a chef, I worked one night in a pizza parlor, then quit in a huff. I've written this experience up both as fiction and nonfiction, reworked it over the years and recently included it a published memoir. Since it's comedy (although it sure didn't seem funny at the time), it's a favorite to read aloud at book signings. By now the story itself is much more real to me than whatever happened at that restaurant so long ago. The fiction stands between me and any real memory of the actual experience. I think we can take a lesson from this when we try to understand what is meant by "story line."

Journaling is for the self, published memoirs for the world, yet one often leads into the other. But it's important to reread our old journals, the ones written without an audience in mind. These unmediated, unedited entries are often closer to the bone than the funny stories about them we tell to others. Occasionally, we all need to circle back around to the source.

Six Word Memoir

A fun exercise to warm up to memoir writing or to do in a group is to try to condense your life so far into six words. When read aloud, it an excellent way to find out about others in the group. One man, a poet, in our workshop wrote:

"Girls. Girls. Girls. Women. Women. Women."

Smith magazine brought out a collection of six-word memoirs of famous and not so famous people called *Not Quite What I Was Planning*. Certainly the title could describe any number of our life stories.

STILL UNSPOKEN

List (perhaps in code) ten things that you would leave out of your memoir.

1.

2.

3.

4.

5.

6.

7.

8.

9.

10.

THE SELF/ NO SELF/ REIFIED SELF

We think we are looking out of a big picture window, but we are really looking at a mirror.

~Lama Tsering Everest

Buddhists often use shorthand for recurrent themes. "No-self," a basic tenet of Buddhism, is short for "You have a self, but it isn't exactly the self you imagine that you have, and furthermore, you don't have it for very long,"

Like the word "emptiness" which can send part of the mind off gibbering in the corner, the term no-self is vastly misunderstood. It doesn't mean that you don't have a self, but that it isn't separate and isolated. Nor it is solid and immutable as we like to think. Nor is it always right. Nor the center of the known universe. The self is an ever-changing, moving collection of aggregates of physical sensations, emotions, thoughts, and consciousness. It is made up of a collage of images concerning our name, gender, nationality, profession, likes, dislikes, and relationships, most of which are updated from time to time. Nonetheless, in the end, it is as cobbled-together and transient as everything else.

In his excellent book, *Stepping Out of Self-Deception*, Rodney Smith points out that our "sense of self" is a functional necessity, but never an abiding reality.

FORMATION OF THE SELF

Things do not exist separately and independently, but are the result of causes and conditions. A flower cannot exist without the sun and the soil, a person cannot come into being without parents. Everything is part of a vast network of interrelated processes. We come into this world as what Tsoknyi Rinpoche calls "the mere I," a capacity to sense, to feel, and to discern. The mere I consists of a fluid sense of being—a stream of experiences, such as warmth and coldness, comfort and discomfort, sleepiness and alertness. At this stage, we have no words or labels for the things we experience or for the self experiencing.

We begin to grow and develop in a world that is a vast interconnected field of ever changing, related factors coming into being and going out of being. Mountains and rivers and skyscrapers, freeways, people and cats and elephants, everything. However, this feels chaotic, so we sort of rope off a section of the huge net and say this is ME, my self, and everything else out there can be seen as the Not-me or Other. This is Kimberley. I'm inside my body. I draw this outline around me with a wide magic marker. The mere I begins to develop into the "solid I."

In the beginning, the "solid I" is pretty much identified with our bodies. In *Open Heart, Open Mind*, Tsoknyi Rinpoche points out that as we mature, this "solid I" becomes more conceptual and abstract:

> It evolves into a sense of separate "I-ness" located somewhere inside our bodies or maybe in our imagination. As we apply tighter, harder labels to our experiences, our thoughts, our emotions, our physical sensations develop a kind of weighty, "thing-like" quality. We begin to identify with our thoughts and feelings as dimensions of experience that are inherently parts of ourselves. As the sense of "I" becomes more solid, the effects of such identification become more powerful and complicated.

At the same time that we assign seemingly true or solid qualities to our selves, a corresponding process begins to evolve through which we assign those same aspects to what or whoever is "not I," or "other." We begin to perceive and to catalog our experiences in terms of friends and enemies; into "things" that we have and "things" that we don't have: "things" that we want and "things" that we don't want.

We begin to enclose the self, grasp on to our ideas about the self, and develop a story line that keeps things in place. For instance, someone may think: I'm a Mac person, I have an iPad, an iPhone, a MacBook Pro. All extensions of ME. My story line is that I know a lot about technology and I have chosen Mac. I am my technology. I look down on people who use a PC, sneer at a Dell. Mac is superior, therefore I am superior.

The problem is that we do this sort of judging with everything and everybody, pulling up evidence from our personal data base rather than relating to the world as it is. All too often this categorizing takes place unconsciously. In a blink we've decided who is worth knowing, what's worth having, and we make the same choices over and over. This can lead to an abstracted, airless quality accompanied by a feeling of being absent from our own lives, and isolated from others.

Paradoxically, when left to itself, our ever-vigilant and over-worked sense of self defends the borders of who we think we are. A great deal of energy goes into judging, then pushing parts of the world away and glomming on to other parts. We can, however, begin to educate our sense of self.

The first step is to create through meditation a tiny gap between our awareness and this hyper-active self. Then let awareness ease it into a dialogue, persuade it to just calm down. Maybe thank it for being as vigilant as a Border Collie, always ready to tighten up the boundaries when it thinks there is danger. Gently explain that no one is at fault here. It's just how things have developed. Relax now, awareness says to the solid sense of self, let me help do the work. Just spend more time sitting in the garden admiring the succulents. Or even consider early retirement. Reading Suggestion:

Open Heart, Open Mind by Tsoknyi Rinpoche. After he describes the formation of the "Mere I" and "Solid I," Rinpoche goes on to name a number of other forms the "I" can take in its development: "The Precious I," "The Social I," and finally, "The Useful I."

EXERCISE: Contemplate the self. As a child. In school, As an adult. Where were you before you were born? Where are you now? Where are you going?

Our Selves

Make a list of your various selves as they exist today that have grown out of your roles or interests:

The social self, worker self, wife, daughter, seeker, dancer, meditator, and so on.

Give them each a name.

Write a scene from a play using three to five of these selves.

Set them around a conference table or kitchen table trying to come to a decision about a current situation in your life or choose one of the following:

You've just received a cash windfall, and are trying to decide how to spend it.

You've just gotten a phone call and your mother/ex-husband/daughter/ is coming to visit. How do the different selves react?

A neighbor has asked for a ride to the airport. One self wants to help her. Another self feels that she should do so, but is conflicted. A third self thinks that there's a good reason why they invented airport pickup cars. The other two are commenting on the situation.

GETTING THE LEAD OUT

Visualize the self as bits of colored glass, each representing aggregate parts such as the body, consciousness, senses, volition and mental activity. See these parts as a piece of stained glass in which leading creates strong borders without and within.

Like the lead that holds the strained glass together, our sense of self grips our edges tightly, holding them in a controlled pattern. If we take away the leading, we haven't lost any of the colored bits of glass, but now instead of being fixed, these essential elements can move, play, dance, like ever-changing patterns in a kaleidoscope.

This grasping onto the edges of a fixed self is often called self-cherishing, but self-defended might be a better translation. We're trying to control our world. We spend a great deal of our time trying to maintain this sense of self. As we've said, we do this through creating categories of what is good, what is bad, what we let in, what we keep out. We codify these likes and dislikes through an ongoing narrative or story line that we tell ourselves. This process leads to the reification of the self, making it seem more real and solid than it is. However, this idea we have about our selves—the one we protect and defend—is no more than a thought that we believe.

When we become aware of this situation, there may be a tendency to see ourselves as a problem that we have to solve. When we hear the teachings about no-self, we may assume that something is wrong with us, that we need to apply another method to ourselves and things will be all right. If this method doesn't work, we may try another teacher, another resource. We get tighter and tighter, more and more intent on solving the problem of the self. But the self can never solve the problem of the self, it always asks the wrong questions. We need to stop looking outside ourselves, need to find the inner stillness that can witness the world with awareness. We need to relax the boundaries of the self, get the lead out, so to speak. We do this through listening to the heart whose voice is softer and more gentle than that of the judging mind's. We need to soften the edges through meditation, dissipate the obscurations of the judging mind by resting in awareness, by surrendering to the wisdom of the heart.

OUR STORYLINE AND THE REIFIED SELF.

> Self-absorption in all its forms kills empathy, let alone compassion. When we focus on ourselves, our world contracts as our problems and preoccupations loom large. But when we focus on others, our world expands. Our own problems drift to the periphery of the mind and so seem smaller, and we increase our capacity for connection - or compassionate action.
>
> ~ Daniel Goleman

Expanding on the stained glass image, one of the key components in the leading that keeps us isolated and frozen in place is the story line itself. Some memoirs try to shore up and reify the self through a sort of hyped up version of the story line. More serious (and more lasting) memoirs are those which attempt to deconstruct a story line in order to come to terms with hidden truths which lie beneath. The same is true when trying to see things just as they are in terms of personal insight.

When we go into the kitchen where dinner is on the stove, we just smell beef stew. A dog comes into the kitchen and separately smells carrots, onions, turnips, meat. The dog knows that the carrots were fresh, the onions had been around for a while and that the meat was over a week old. When you're looking into your storyline, be like the dog.

Read your journals: find your story line. Be honest about what happened and whether your commentary is skewed by age, partial knowledge, or the need to protect yourself. Don't see the story line as a bad thing. It just is. What's needed is to recognize the narrative for what it is and to track its effect. It isn't that the story line didn't happen; often it can be quite factual. But it is only a partial truth. What other things happened? What isn't being included? Is anything being denied, rejected, covered over, ignored?

See how your story line changes, how it doesn't change. Be aware of how you shape the story line around different events. Sniff it all out.

WRITING: The Reified "I"

Make a list of the objects in your life (car, job title, designer labels, etc.) that contribute to the reification of your sense of self.

Make a list of the people in your life that enhance your sense of self.

Make a list of people and things that challenge your sense of self.

INVENT A PERSONA

Create a character from some aspect of your own personality. Maybe draw on a younger self. Or someone you hope(d) to become. Switch genders if you wish. Give he/she a name. A profession, an attitude, a storyline.

Or create a persona, using personality elements very unlike your own. A biker. A Zen monk. An alien.

Write a journal entry from their point of view.

OR

Write (a poem, flash fiction, etc.) about this person.

OTHER PEOPLE

Two things to remember:

You are not the story line people create about you.

Other people are not the story line you make up about them.

GOING DEEPER

Spiritual realization is relatively easy compared with the much greater difficulty of actualizing it, integrating it fully into the fabric of one's daily life. Realization is the movement from personality to being, the direct recognition of one's ultimate nature, leading toward liberation from the conditioned self, while actualization refers to how we integrate that realization in all the situations of our life.

~John Welwood

What both Freud and Jung called `the unconscious' is simply what we, in our historically conditioned estrangement, are unconscious of. It is not necessarily or essentially unconscious.

~R. D. Laing

TAKING CARE OF YOURSELF

We talk of the need to take care of ourselves, but too often focus on the outward ways to do this: a walk in the woods, a hot bath, an afternoon movie. We can get quite precious and precise in our self-care: a pedicure, new bedding, more jewelry. This can easily slide into sheer indulgence and clinging which creates a kind of craving. We think *this* is going to work to make us feel better. But *this* is never enough. It turns out to be the wrong size, the wrong color, leaving a sense of dissatisfaction in the project of self care. So we keep looking, keep piling up things and experiences that enhance our sense of self.

The ultimate way to take care of ourselves is to understand how our mind works, to be mindful how it is setting us up for misery and a sense of isolation, how it creates causes and conditions that makes it impossible to access core happiness.

Core happiness is innate, the right of every sentient creature, but it needs to be uncovered and it's surroundings often need to go through a sort of detox. One of the quickest ways is to meditate on essence love, to find that little spark within containing the seeds of the positive emotions of love, compassion, joy and equanimity. Locate that feeling of okayness somewhere in the heart region and simply connect with it, at first touch it lightly, don't pounce. You don't need your head for this, it isn't a thought about a feeling, but a feeling itself. Simply feel the connections without skittering around. Link to it.

LEARN HOW YOUR MIND WORKS

> It is a very remarkable thing how ideas come into a mind, or minds: one minute we are thinking this or that, as if no other thought is possible to us; shortly after, there are quite different beliefs, dispossessing the old ones, and to be dispossessed, of course, soon enough in their turn.

> ~Doris Lessing

When we begin to watch our mind, we uncover a number of obstacles that keep us separate from our deeper selves, thus from our creativity.

According to Buddhist psychology, there are three root things that poison the mind: attachment, aversion and ignorance. This isn't a moral failing on our part that we have these veils covering over our deeper nature. It comes with being embodied, with our human nature. Until we start to look under the hood of the mind, so to speak, this responding automatically is our default mode.

Often unconsciously when we see something, we tend to want it, push it away, or be neutral. When we want it, we reach out toward it to grasp it, in a light or heavy manner, we attach ourselves to it. Or we see it, don't want it, push it away. In addition, we make judgments about it. It's good, it's bad.

And ignorance? It's the basis of both of the above. Ignorance is indulging in attachment and aversion, in not knowing any better, in thinking the duality (self and other, for instance) we create in our own minds is real, solid, firm. Which it isn't. What we think of as our self isn't real either. Not that it isn't there. Something's there, but it's changing, coming into being, going out of being, each instant.

Furthermore, the self—myself, yourself, himself—is like the weather. Not real or solid, but happening. Sometimes the rain and hail dominate everything. Other times, the clouds are light and fluffy, lots of sky showing through. But it's always impermanent, always changing, never the same from minute to minute. The sky behind the clouds doesn't change, but often we can't see the sky because of the cloud cover.

How do we get out of this? The first thing to do is to learn not to identify with our immediate response, just watch our thoughts, our emotions, our crazy reactions. Don't do anything. Just witness the mind from somewhere just outside of it. Don't think about watching the mind, just watch it. This takes time. Be patient.

After we are able to watch our mind and its antics, we can get in dialogue with it. Perhaps the first thing we need to say is: "Honey, we have to talk."

One thing you'll notice as you watch the mind, as you relate to it in a different way is that the part of you (your awareness) that is watching the mind is neither in the past nor the future, but in the present. If we can get a whiff of the present, we can learn to sniff it out again and again for longer and longer periods of time. As we learn to identify with this sense of presence in the present, our identification with that busy-busy fountain of thoughts bubbling up begins to lessen, but also we begin to feel a sense of peace and frissons of joy. Inner peace is spontaneously present in the now, as is wisdom and compassion. We're not giving up a thing when we quit paying so much attention to our busy brain. On the contrary, we are learning to use our minds in a new way.

That's why we meditate, in order to dis-identify with the busy brain and develop true awareness. Meditation is a sort of super highway toward understanding the way the mind works. All religious traditions have a method of meditation although it is most often associated with Buddhism. Even atheists can meditate. But that doesn't mean that it is always easy. Nonetheless, it's worth the trouble to learn how to do it.

If you find the idea of meditation overly complicated or too foreign, just sit there quietly and breathe.

BE AWARE OF DUALISTIC MIND

> Unfortunately our Western mind, lacking all culture in this respect, has never yet devised a concept, nor even a name, for the 'union of opposites through the middle path,' that most fundamental item of inward experience, which could respectably be set against the Chinese concept of the Tao.

> ~Carl G. Jung

Our mind is conditioned first because we are humans who have a specific configuration of the brain, fed information via neurons and synapses, via the five senses. It is further conditioned by the language we speak. In the West, it is probably English with its bent toward dualism dividing things into twos: subject-object, right-left, you-me. This type of dualism is built in and is so common that it seems inevitable. Nonetheless, we should be aware that there is a lot of middle out there.

I came to some conclusions about dualism while making a chocolate mousse which I later wrote up as:

Transcending Dualism
While Whipping Egg Whites into High Stiff Peaks

Working at the restaurant, I'd think a lot about the topic of my dissertation on feminism and dualism which I didn't have time to write. One day when making a chocolate mousse, I'd carefully separated the yolks from the whites, putting them each in their own identical grey bowls, fat yellow moons and a little glaucous sea. Gently sprinkled sugar over the thick, rich yellows, adding dark chocolate melted with butter. As I stirred, the egg mixture darkened, thickened. I whipped the whites in the other bowl until they stood frothy and unspotted, the purest white. In contrast, the container of dense chocolate seemed laden with the dark sexuality of some brooding seducer in a _fin de siecle_ drawing.

Visually, at least, the contents of the two bowls loomed up as

124

opposites, as yin and yang, one light, dry, the other dark, heavy, wet. But which should be called the male, which the female? I'd seen the white purity as virginal female, but in Taoism, the woman would be aligned with the wet darkness of yin. If we go from West to East, do we switch the alignments of masculine and feminine? And what of the values attributed to each side? Would the passivity and maschocism the Freudians assigned to women in the West, be seen as Eastern virtues of equanimity and compassion? And then? What else would change? Everything?

As I moved on to the final step of combining the mousse, folding the heavy brown globs into the stark purity of the egg whites. the commingled mixture took on its own creamy texture in a willing seduction, came an orgy of pleasures as the dark entered the whites and the envaginated light penetrated and enfolded and merged with the dark.

Soon I'd forgotten about opposites altogether, disappearing into the action. Mixing, remembering how men and women merge as seamlessly as yin and yang become the Tao. Mixing, understanding why the union of man and woman goes beyond thought of self and other.

Mixing, mingling. Skin on skin, fur on fur, tongue on nipple. Goatleg sliding goatleg. Down, backward, falling though the trapdoors of self, into the river of male and female together. . . loving, mating, bonding without thought of hesitation, no more able to keep separate boundaries than the egg whites and the chocolate coming together in shared wetness and fecundity could ever again live apart.

I understood then that it didn't matter which side is called masculine, which feminine, but as long as I viewed them as opposites, I'd continue to create—and strive to overcome—dualism after dualism. Only when I disappeared into the action, when I myself became the mixing, enfolding dark into white, did I free myself from a sense of separation, opposition, alienation.

For a long while after that every time I'd try to theorize about feminism and dualism, my thoughts would still harden and turn grey, like chocolate that been left too long in the cold. But I understood it all that afternoon in the hot restaurant kitchen.

Then the dreams started. Every night I dreamed a pattern of two, three, five. Two lanterns would turn into three lanterns, then five and, almost immediately, multiple lights. Two flowers would become three, five, a field. It took me a while to realize the dream code beneath the images, but it kept repeating night after night until I finally noticed.

But what did it mean? I had the feeling that nightly my unconscious was waving to me—all but shouting yoohoo—with the way out of dualism. If the dream had stopped at three, I would have been fine: thesis, antithesis, synthesis. I'd quoted Hegel enough to have him show up nightly in my dreams, but what was with the five, then multiplicity? That the Hegelian dialectic extended to an endless loop that the Western mind kept getting stuck in?

In one particularly vivid dream, the two and threes were clouds. When I got to the multiplicity part that night, for the first time I noticed not the number of clouds, but the sky behind them.

When I went into the sky, I felt a sense not only of opening into vastness, but of being connected with everything contained within it. That's what my dreams had been trying to tell me. Not the figure, but the ground. Non-dual at last. And this was before I started studying Buddhism, but one of a series of hints, messages that my unconscious kept sending me

WRITING: Contemplate dualism, take two opposing words/concepts, personify them, give them names and put them in dialogue with each other as they explore the large grey area between them. Look over your journals and other writing. Sniff out examples of dualistic thinking.

PAY ATTENTION TO LANGUAGE

Language uses us as much as we use language.

~Robin Lakoff

In addition to the ways in which our thinking is influenced by the structure of a language, our minds are further changed and conditioned by the way in which we have personally customized the language in which we think and operate. Certain words we associate with things that have brought us pleasure sort of glow at us. Just saying them makes us happy: these might include California, blue velvet, truffles, husband. Others words and phrases we associate with pain—chemotherapy, fired, divorce, *husband*—might be among them. These we distrust, push away, stiffen up around.

Our experience of the world is shaped by the language we use to describe it. In turn this shapes and is shaped by the way we perceive ourselves and our place in the world, so pay attention to language itself, to the way certain words or phrases can be used to reify ideas or concepts. Focus on the way in which language sometimes drives us into smaller and smaller boxes.

MEDITATION: find a spot that is non-verbal and hang out there for a while.

127

FIND A MODERN MANTRA

Don't do mantra, let it happen to you.

~Ram Dass

A mantra is a sound, syllable, word, or group of words that is called a "mind protector" in Tibetan Buddhism. Traditionally, mantras were tied to certain deities and mainly chanted in Sanskrit, but today, their type and use varies widely.

One thing any mantra does is to jump the track from obsessive thoughts to a repetition of a phrase that might prove helpful. It keeps us from digging in with the obsessive thoughts and allows us to pause and clear the mind through focusing on something else.

Many of us already have a mantra such as "Oh shit," or something similar that we say under stress. An intentional mantra is probably a better idea.

A personal mantra can be used as a social survival skill. "Don't say it, don't say it, don't say it" can be useful in many a situation. Sometimes a line from a song can become a personal mantra. "Let it be" is a good one.

Others have found these mantras powerful:

"That was then, this is now."

"Don't go there."

"Life's too short."

"I've resigned from that committee."

"I choose not to have an opinion about that."

"What would love do now?"

"Let things just be as they are."

"Love More."

Tsoknyi Rinpoche, in *Open Heart, Open Mind* describes a situation in which he felt panic when trying to cross a glass bridge between two buildings. Even though he rationally knew that his fear was fed by past experiences of falling out of a tree when a child and further fueled by terrifying plane rides in the mountains of Nepal, he couldn't make himself cross the glass bridge. He finally said to himself, "It feels real, but it isn't true." When he began repeating "real, but not true; real but not true; real but not true," he was able to finally cross the bridge.

Create a mantra for yourself. Remember a time you were in a conflicted situation and found a solution. Try to formulate that solution into a single phrase that you can repeat in future. The phrases that arise spontaneously are generally the ones that you remember and use, but others, like "real, but not true," can be adapted.

LOVE MORE

The thought manifests as the word

The word manifests as the deed

The deed develops into habit

Habit hardens into character

So watch the thought and its ways with care

And let it spring out of love

Born out of concern for all beings

As the shadow follows the body as we think, so we become.

~Shakyamuni Buddha

Start small. Find something that spontaneously creates a genuine feeling of love in your heart. Maybe your dog. Dwell on this feeling. You don't have to give it more treats or pet it more, but let the feeling expand outward. Love the cat.

Maybe it is a plant. Succulents are easy to fall in love with—they are very cooperative, very low maintenance, can survive almost anything and thrive. They reproduce without being asked, mind their own business and throw out beautifully wild blossoms from time to time. Extend this sense of affection and gratitude to other living things, to all of nature.

People are a little more problematic, so start with babies. Try to get in the grocery line behind someone with a baby. Look into the sweet innocence of its face, so open to the world. Remember that every person you meet was once a baby.

In time, you might fall in love with the world. What's to stop you?

SEEK CORE HAPPINESS

We might assume that happiness comes from the outside and that if only the world would shape up and do things the way we want, we'd be happy. Of if we had more money or a different wife or a bigger house, or if our daughter just wouldn't act that way, if she just hadn't married that man, then we'd be really happy.

Much of this type of thinking is unconscious and unexamined. It is perhaps a calcified remnant of a very primitive or childish ego that needs to be dissolved or chipped away before we can be grown-up human beings who are able to relate to others in a meaningful way. Sometimes life and maturity will do this for us, but consciously conditioning the mind speeds things up. Meditation is a good way to soften and dissolve this false view, and contemplation is an excellent method for chipping it away.

Core happiness is found within by realizing the potential of our own hearts and minds, not through what we own or what we do. It's already there, we just need to learn to tap into it.

We pursue pleasure as we've been taught to do, but we get caught on a hedonic treadmill, and gerbil-like spend our days going faster and faster, hoping to find happiness.

Turn inward instead. Let happiness catch up with you.

BE HELPFUL

> If we have no peace, it is because we have forgotten that
> we belong to each other.
>
> ~Mother Teresa

A good habit to develop is a simple one: when you enter a room, any room, ask yourself: what can I do to help? How can I make things better? In time, this habit can gradually change your life. And the life of those around you.

UNDERSTANDING OBSTACLES

AND OBSCURATIONS

Sometimes during the process of awakening, it isn't what we do that is important nearly as much as what we stop doing. But first, of course, we have to be conscious of the patterns and habits that keep us fixated within the dream of self. Writing, contemplation, and meditation all help to bring these things into consciousness.

As we have said, emotions, ideas, memories and feelings become fused together in our personal data base, and when a situation begins to repeat, fused emotions and memories are imported into the present situation, recreating it. The more this happens, the deeper the rut; the deeper the rut, the less chance of a new response. If there was a repeated occurrence of rejection in our childhood, for instance, when we approach a situation which feels similar, our automatic appraisal system names and reacts to it so quickly that we don't even know this is happening. If, in turn, our ingrained reaction to rejection serves to shut us down or become defensive, then our withdrawal from what could have been a pleasant encounter is felt by the other person as indifference, who now turns away. Another rejection.

For instance, at a retreat I coordinated, I was carrying a tray of food to the tea table when a woman stepped in front of me. She told me how upset she was that someone had walked away from her as she was talking. She went on to say that this happened to her a great deal. In her own family, there were two older boys who got all of the attention and she had the feeling that no one wanted her around. The tray in my hands was getting heavier and heavier, but she talked on and on about her hurt feelings. As politely as possible, I told her I was sorry, but....She looked stricken, walked away with tears in her eyes. I never got to mention the need to put down the tray or the fact that I had a great deal still to do before the morning session began. She withdrew, rejected yet again. Proof positive.

When these self-perpetuating patterns are especially intense, when they seem to come out of nowhere to roar forth and emotionally highjack a situation, they are called *kleshas* in Tibetan Buddhism. The word is variously translated as compulsions, afflicted emotions, and distorted mind states. Therapists refer to them as complexes, but whatever they are called, they cause us a lot of trouble. The good news from both traditional Buddhists and from current neuroscientists is that we can change these patterns by training the brain.

EXERCISE: Become mindful of a pattern that has caused you (and probably others) grief. Watch for it in action.

WORKING WITH THE MESSY STUFF

> To be happy, to me, is to suffer less. If we were not capable of transforming the pain within ourselves, happiness would not be possible.
>
> ~ Thich Nhat Hanh

While meditation in the West has come to mean relaxation and serenity, in traditional Buddhism, the range is much wider and the intent more geared toward permanent change rather than simple relaxation. In fact, "good" meditation includes periods of chaos and distress.

If we wish to include insight into process, the first step is to establish mental stability through calm abiding meditation, following the breath or just sitting. Next, simply observe what arises in the mind without doing anything about it. Just watch. As we all know, things do arise, some positive and some connected to afflicted mind states – jealousy, doubt, contempt, judging, anger—the list goes on and on.* Make a conscious decision which one you'd like to work on. The others don't go away, but will wait their turn. For the present, simply pick one afflicted or distorted mind state, major or minor, to delve into.

The second step is to create objectivity. You are not it—not the anger, not the jealousy—but a witness to it and its effects on your life. Thich Nhat Hanh says:

> Mindfulness is the capacity of being aware of what is going on in the present moment. "Breathing in, I know that anger has manifested in me; breathing out, I smile towards my anger." This is not an act of suppression or of fighting. It is an act of recognizing. Once we recognize our anger, we embrace it with a lot of awareness, a lot of tenderness.

To gain insight, try to understand both the emotion itself and also the way it has played out in your life. What are the triggers? What are the roots of the triggers? Where did they start? How did it become

135

a habit? At this point, you remain in a field of stillness as a fall back, but your attention is focused on gaining insight into the afflicted mind state rather than staying in calm abiding meditation. Don't feel that you "aren't meditating" when you do not stay with following the breath. This is a different type of meditation, called Vipassana, and the intent is to gain insight into your mind and emotions. It goes hand and hand with calm abiding to create changes which can eventually lead to paradigm shifts.

Remember that emotions exist in relationship to each other and that they are tied to interactions with other people. Try to be as objective as possible about others as well. Investigate the story line, the narrative that you tell yourself.

In time, through meditation you can develop what is called the "witness" which is a no-praise/no-blame way of looking at things that illuminates the whole without being analytical. "Like a flash of lightening on a dark night."

It is important to recognize when to stop. If it gets too intense to bear, go back to stillness and breathe. Since there are layers and layers of distortion, the process is slow and often painful. Don't be faint-hearted. Often you'll dissolve one layer to find a different one behind it. Fear might mask anger or vice versa. At first you might be dealing with symptoms and not root causes. Keep going.

Sometimes, just leave it alone and apply an antidote: for instance, switch to a loving kindness meditation to counteract anger.

A very important step is to stitch together insights gained in meditation with your post-meditation life. You can use the insights to reinforce the affliction or to dissolve it. For instance, through meditation, you can discover the ways in which you've been badly treated. In post-meditation you can use this to reinforce your sense of someone who is wounded or you can use it to develop forgiveness or compassion for others who have been mistreated. Up to you.

The final step in dealing with afflicted mind states through meditation, is to rejoice when you've been successful in understanding something about your situation, Make it a point to rejoice when you've gained even a small liberation. Rich Hanson and other neuroscientists have said that we change the brain's bias toward negativity when we dwell on the positive. "What fires together, wires together." In going through this process over and over we are able to change afflicted mental states and transform our lives.

*One Buddhist text states: "The six primary afflictive emotions are desire-attachment, anger, pride, ignorance, opinionatedness and indecision. The twenty secondary afflictive emotions include hatred, resentment, evasiveness, spite, pretense, dishonesty, jealousy-envy, avarice, arrogance, malice, shamelessness, impropriety, depression agitation, lack of faith, laziness, recklessness, forgetfulness, distractedness and inattentiveness."

I am indebted to Venerable Tenzin Priyadarshi for the above sequencing, given at a retreat in Santa Barbara, June, 2014.

RESOURCES:

Thich Nhat Hanh, *Anger,* 2001.

Dalai Lama & Daniel Goleman, *Destructive Emotions, How can We Overcome Them?* 2000.

Daniel Goleman, *Emotional Intelligence: Why It Can Matter More Than Intelligence,* 2005.

PODCASTS: for an extremely helpful treatment of different afflicted or distorted mind states, see Rodney Smith's podcast series at http://seattleinsight.org/

Distortions of the Mind 1, 2, & 3 Series from 2002.

INTEGRATING INSIGHTS FROM THE CUSHION

As we said, the list of distorted or afflictive mind states is long and probably all too familiar. It includes jealousy, pride, arrogance, depression, craving, and grasping. Our minds can be shaped by being overly judging, controlling, doubting, driven, revengeful, distracted, melancholy, worried, speedy, indulgent, disconnected, flighty, indecisive, shameful, guilt-ridden, controlling, Take your pick.

WRITING: select one of your top three afflictive states and write about it in terms of real estate. Give it a name: The Hungry Ghost Mall, the Mansion of Pride, the Slough of Despond, the Fortress of Defensiveness. Describe it in detail, how it came to be built, the function it served, what it keeps in, what it keeps out. Explore it. Then find a way out.

The trick is to be interested in it rather than simply trying to destroy it. Be gentle with it, with yourself, with the pattern that has grown up.

MINDFULNESS: For two weeks, keep a diary of one of the distorted mind states. It doesn't even have to be the most bothersome. Note what triggers the mind state, how quickly it kicks in, how soon you become aware of it. Investigate how many different emotions are involved; often one will be hiding behind another or hidden inside of it. Record the reaction in your body (knots in the stomach, etc.) as well as how you are affected emotionally. Do you shut down? Become aggressive? See if paying close attention to the state lessens the refractory period or allows you to stop or lessen it before it begins.

Once you've become acutely aware of the way competition, arrogance, judging, etc. affects your life in a negative way, make the intention to give it up for one week. It's like going on a diet: no competition for a week. The intention does wonders to alert you to your habitual thought pattern and to allow you to create a gap before you act it out. In your diary, note what happens to you when you choose an alternative way of thinking. Note down the reactions of those around you. Is there a sense of liberation and ease? Try it again for a second week.

DEVELOP EQUANIMITY

> When we start to prefer our own children over other
> people's, war is not far behind.
> ~ The Mahabaratha

Equanimity is more than just calmness, but denotes an even hand-ed approach to all things. It is sometimes translated as "to see with patience" and allows a person to see things just as they are, without projection, without the see-saw of hope and fear. It is not to be con-fused with *indifference* which is often called its facsimile or near enemy.

Another element of equanimity comes from inner balance. The strong presence of inner calm, well-being, confidence, vitality, or integrity can keep us upright, like a ballast keeps a ship upright in strong winds. As inner strength develops, equanimity follows. These work together: We become mindful of things just as they are and are able to stay calm in the face of this.

Equanimity comes naturally with age, but you don't have to wait that long. Start now with clear seeing and being less reactive.

PRACTICE PRESENCE

> Let us recall that the "nature of things" is for us the best, the most affectionate, and the most humiliating of masters; it surrounds us with vigilant assistance. The only task incumbent upon us is to understand reality and to let ourselves be transformed by it.
>
> ~Hubert Benoit

Presence is simply showing up and paying attention, yet it can be surprisingly difficult to maintain for a sustained period of time.

Calm abiding meditation cultivates presence by training the mind to keep coming back to the breath. Take this a step further in daily life and keep bringing yourself back to the present moment without distraction. To do this in a conversation means that you listen deeply to what the other is saying. To focus on a task without your mind wandering away is also a way of being present.

"What doing, do," was the succinct way Chagdud Tulku Rinpoche expressed this to his students. In fact, we had this written large on the kitchen wall of his retreat center.

BE A FLOWER

At a retreat on aging, someone told the Buddhist teacher that her sister, who had never meditated but had lived a very secular, materialistic life, now had dementia. The person said that she wanted to help her sister, maybe teach her to meditate, and asked the teacher how she should proceed.

He thought for a minute, then told the woman to go and spend time with her sister, but not as a teacher. "Go as a flower," he said. "Be something beautiful for her to enjoy."

Next Saturday, all day, everywhere you go, be a flower.

Write a Death Poem

The Japanese tradition of writing a death poem began with Zen monks, but was also popular with poets. Considered a gift to loved ones, students and friends left behind, the tone varied from flippant to serious. The poems often use symbols of death, such as the full moon, the western sky, the song of the cuckoo, and images from the season in which the writer died.

They say that the moment of death can be terrifying, especially when it comes suddenly and one is unprepared. No one wakes up in the morning and thinks, today I will die in an accident, today I'll be murdered, but one never knows. So prepare. In order to meet death consciously and with a composed mind, start by writing a death poem.

Here's one written in a recent writing and meditation workshop in Santa Barbara.

> The leaf
>
> yellow and curled
>
> falls from the tree
>
> without fear
>
> Jane Eagleton

Some teachers suggest that you begin each day with a death poem. A lawyer in Los Angeles similarly advises his clients to write a death poem each day while going through a divorce.

REST IN AWARENESS

Rest the mind throughout the day by simply relaxing it. You don't need to find a quiet spot or get out your cushion or set the clock. Simply stop what you are doing and let the mind expand into open presence. No center, no circumference. No alteration, no contrivance. Suchness.

Made in the USA
San Bernardino, CA
30 January 2016